This book belongs to a great artist

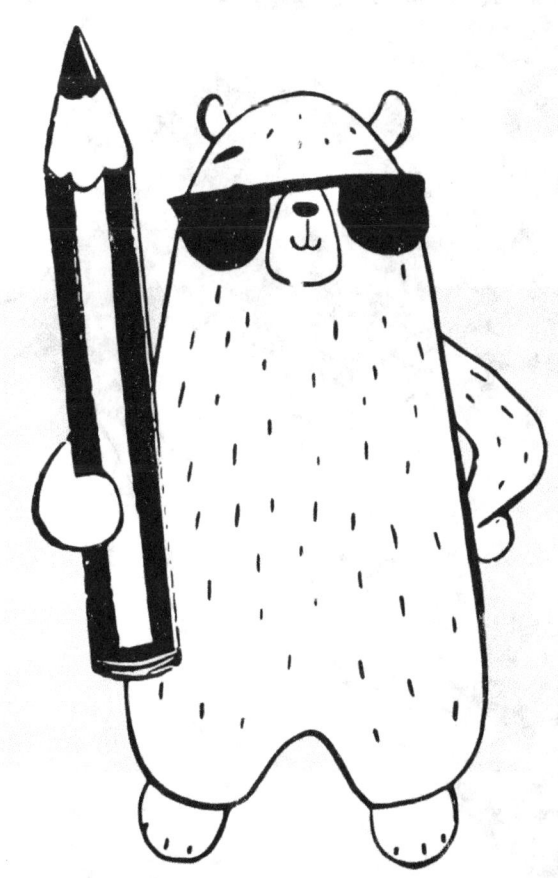

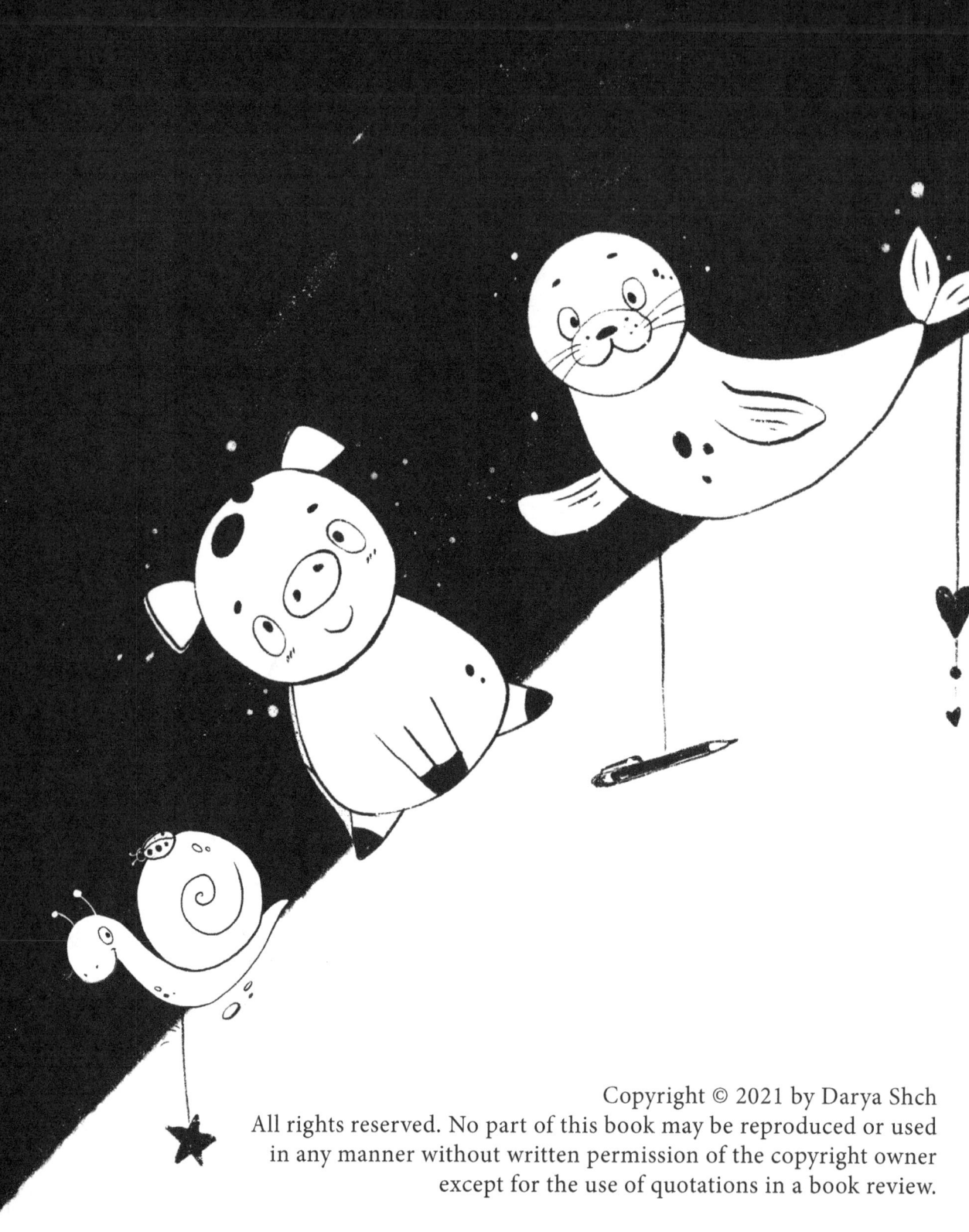

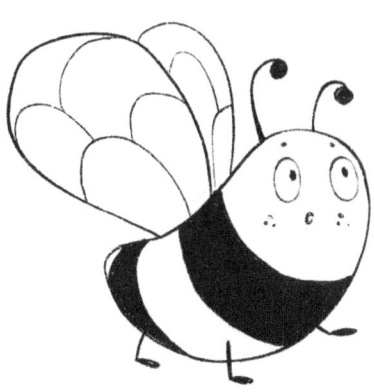

CUTE
ANIMALS
AND HOW TO DRAW THEM

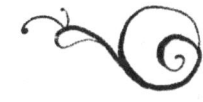

by Darya Shch

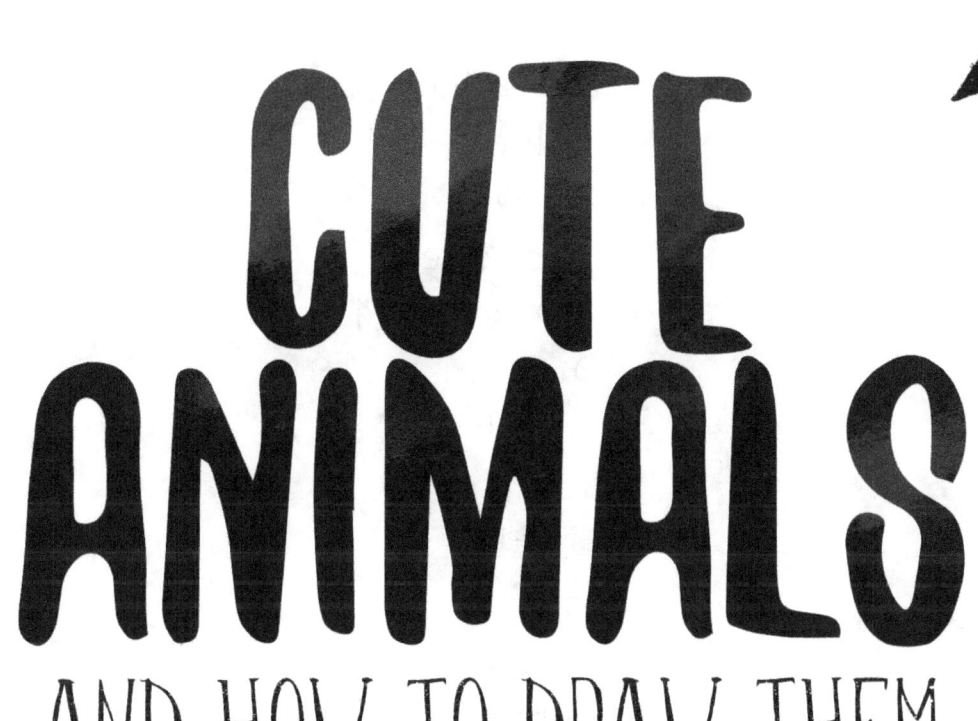

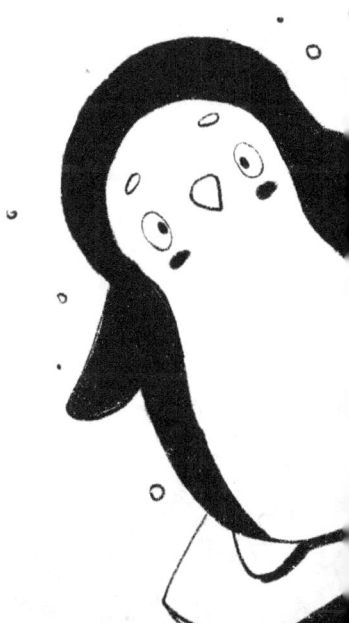

Animals

Tips

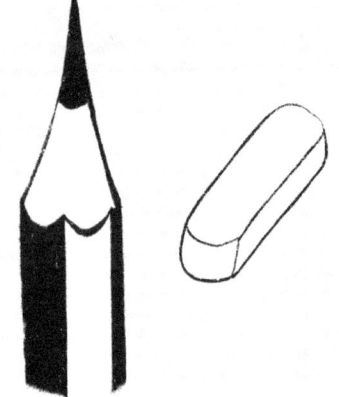

Start with a sharp pencil and
a rubber, so you're not afraid to make
mistakes.

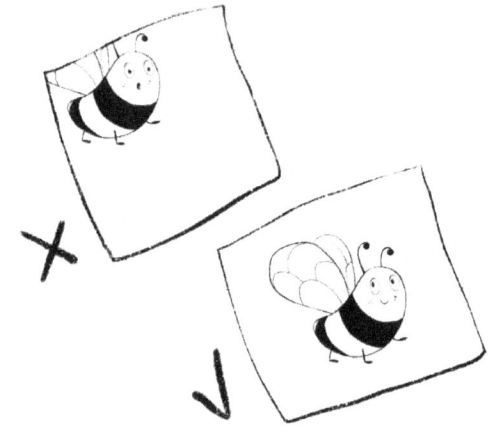

Look carefully at all the steps before
you start drawing and plan some space
on your paper for the entire animal.

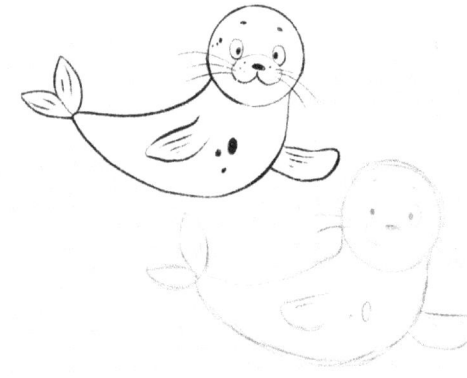

Try to start with very light lines and add
the weight when you get comfortable.

Don't be afraid of imperfection - they make your drawings unique!

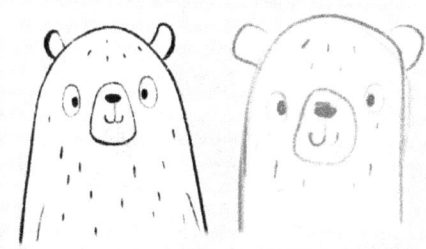

Get creative and add more details! Copy the original or come up with your own ideas!

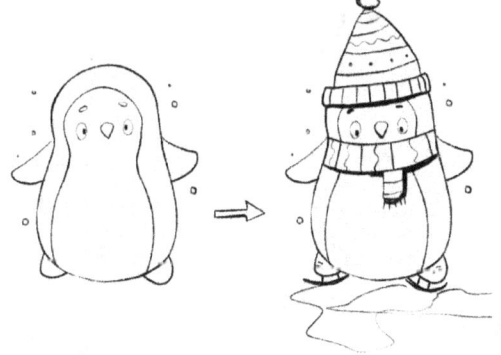

Once you've learned how to draw someone, you can create an entire family for them!

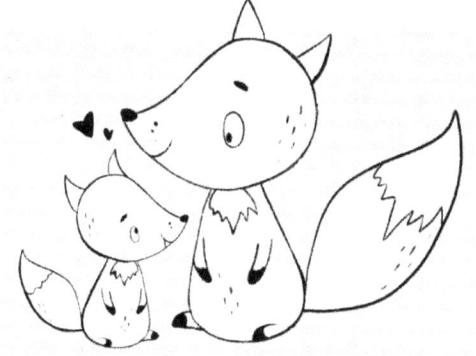

Enjoy!

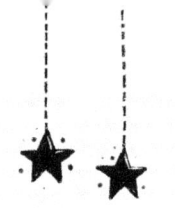

Bear

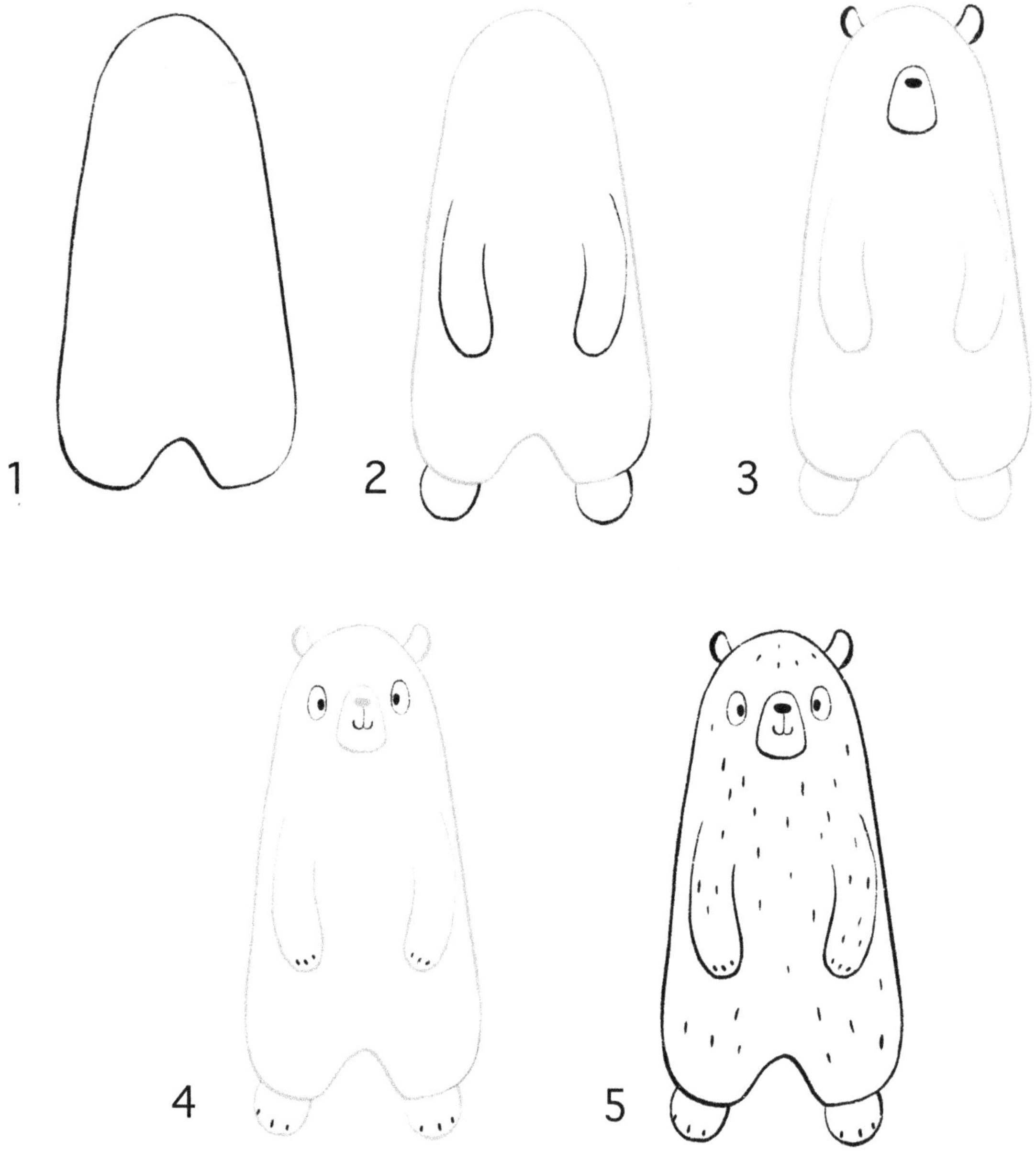

1

2

3

4

5

Practice here!

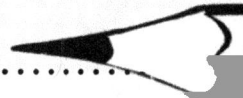

Make a polar bear or a grizzly bear!

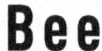

Bee

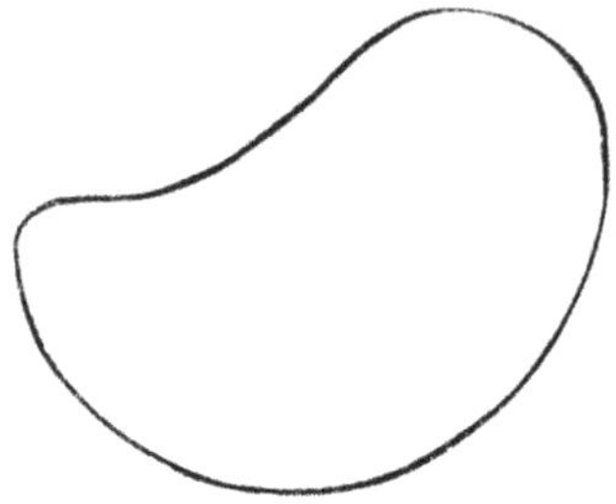

1

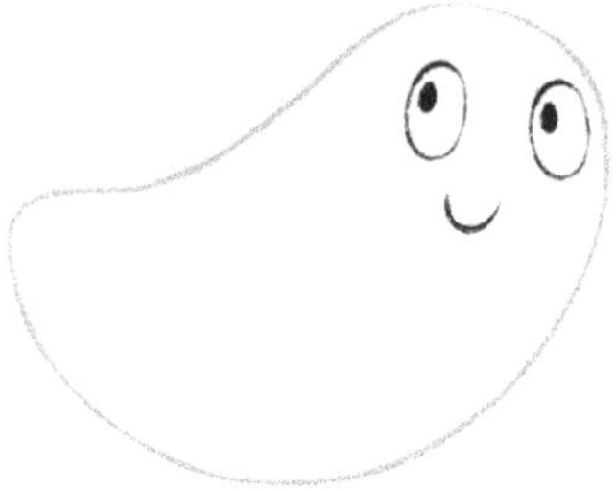

2

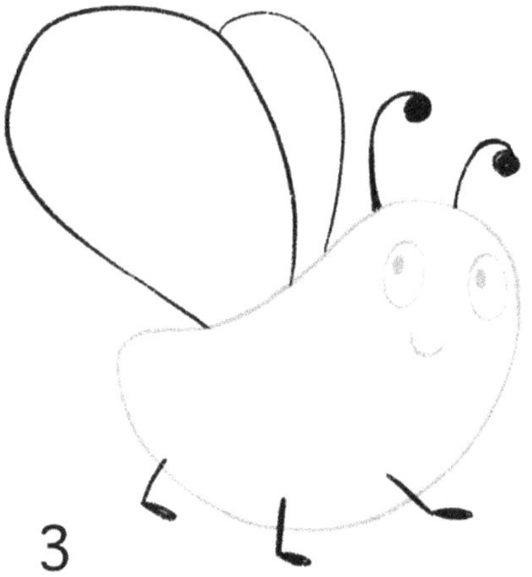

3

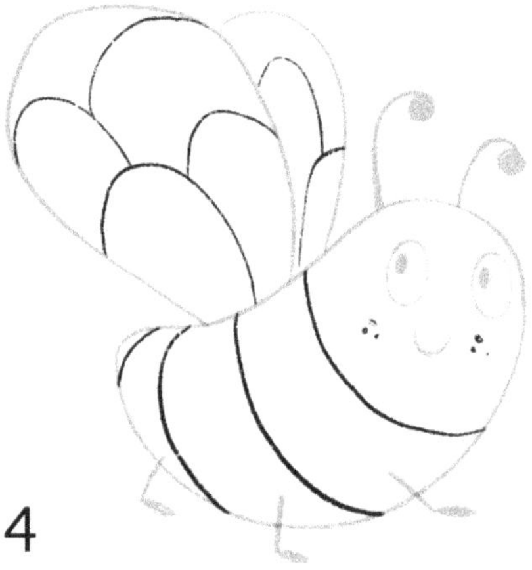

4

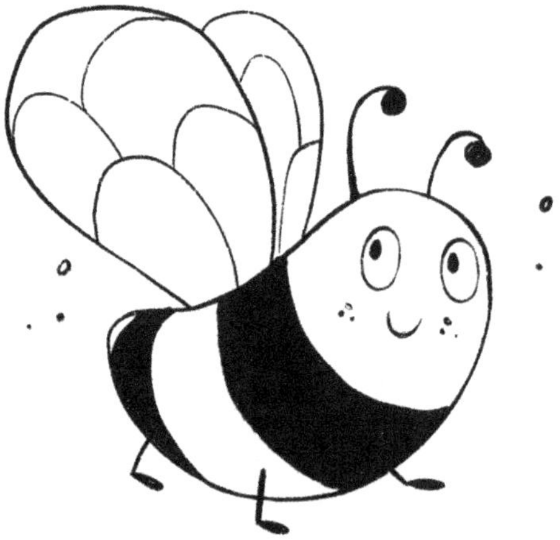

5

8

Practice here!

Draw a queen bee!

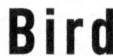

Bird

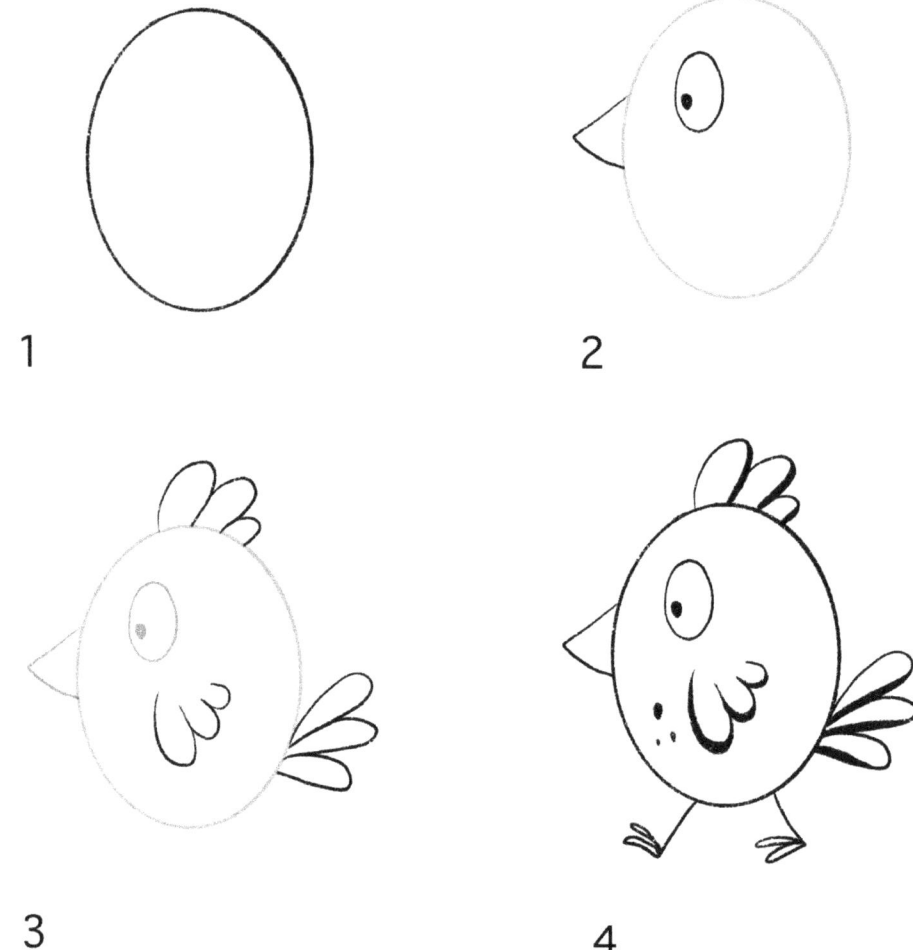

1

2

3

4

Practice here!

Butterfly

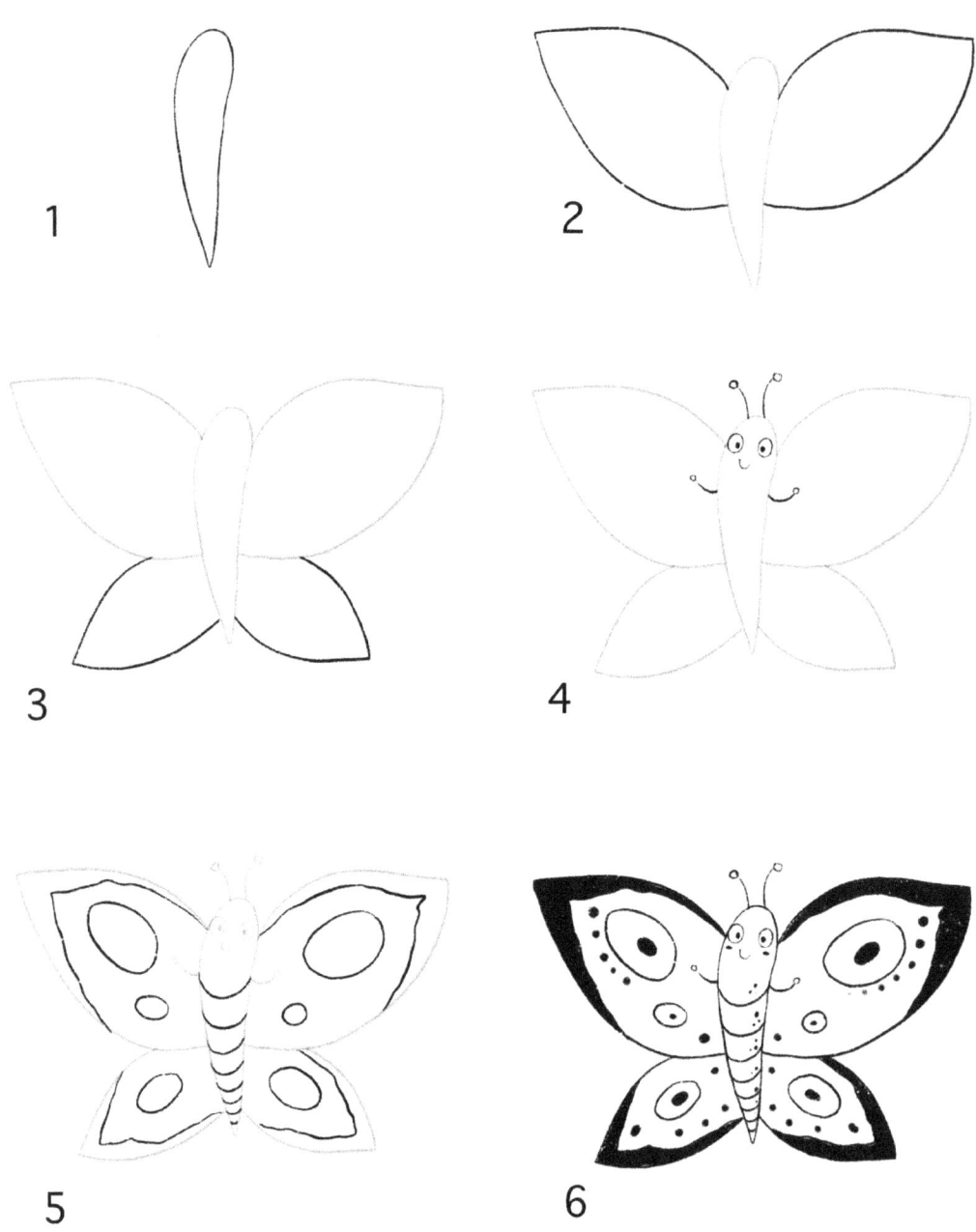

1

2

3

4

5

6

12

Practice here!

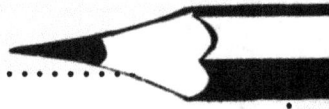

Try different shapes and patterns for the wings!

Cat

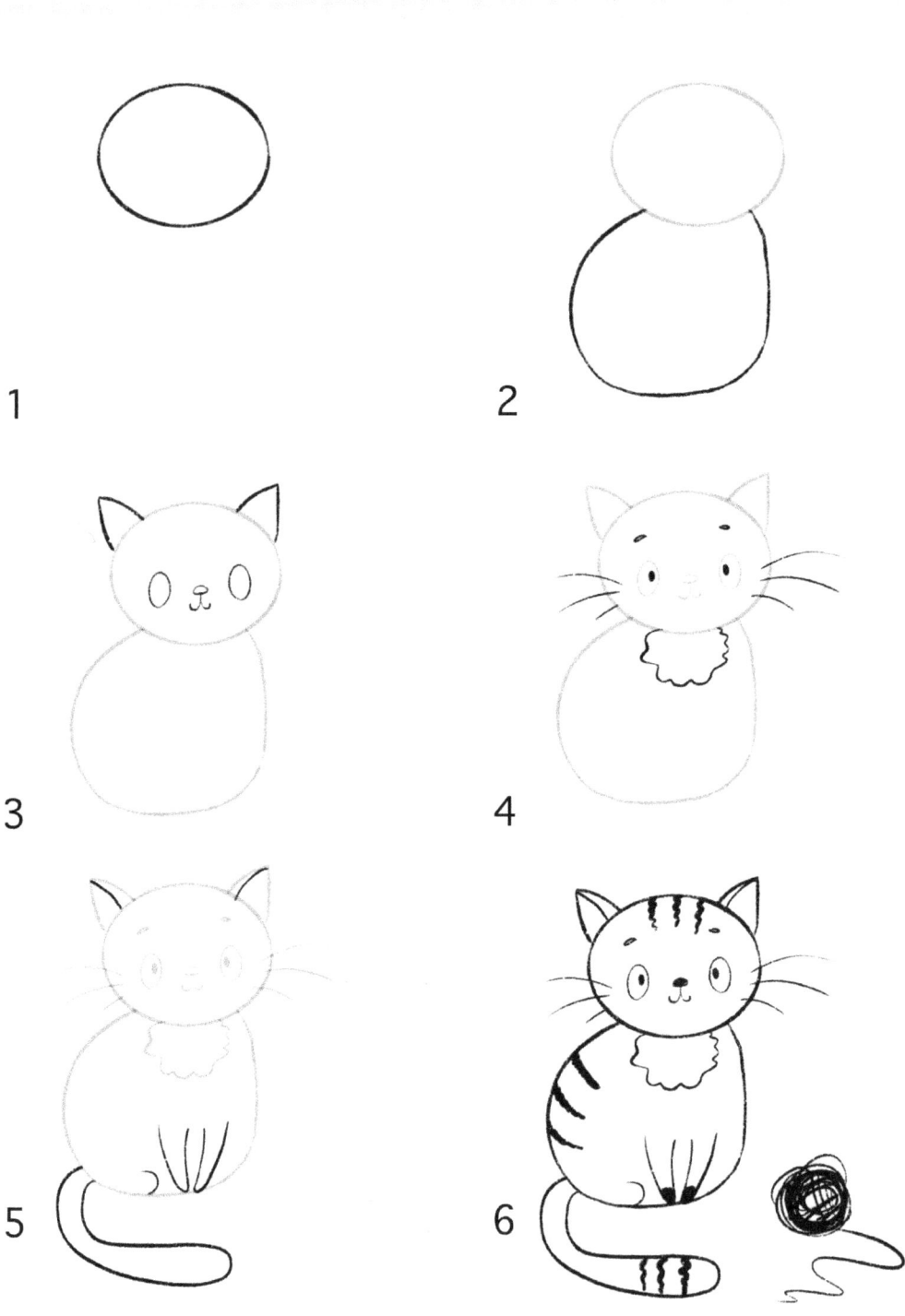

1

2

3

4

5

6

Practice here!

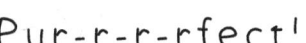

Pur-r-r-rfect!

Caterpillar

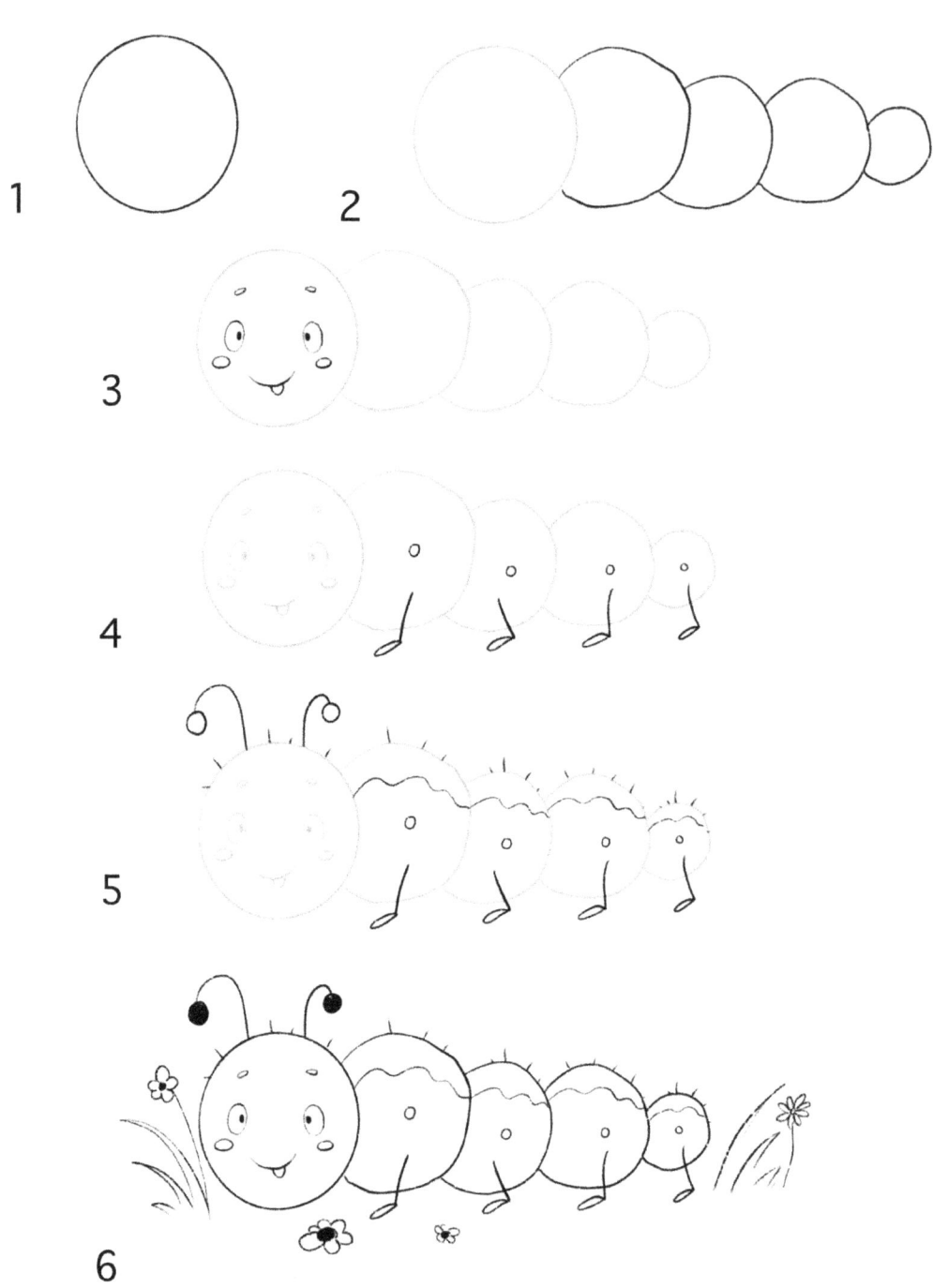

1

2

3

4

5

6

Practice here!

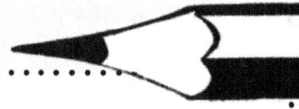

Imagine drawing shoes for her..?

Chick

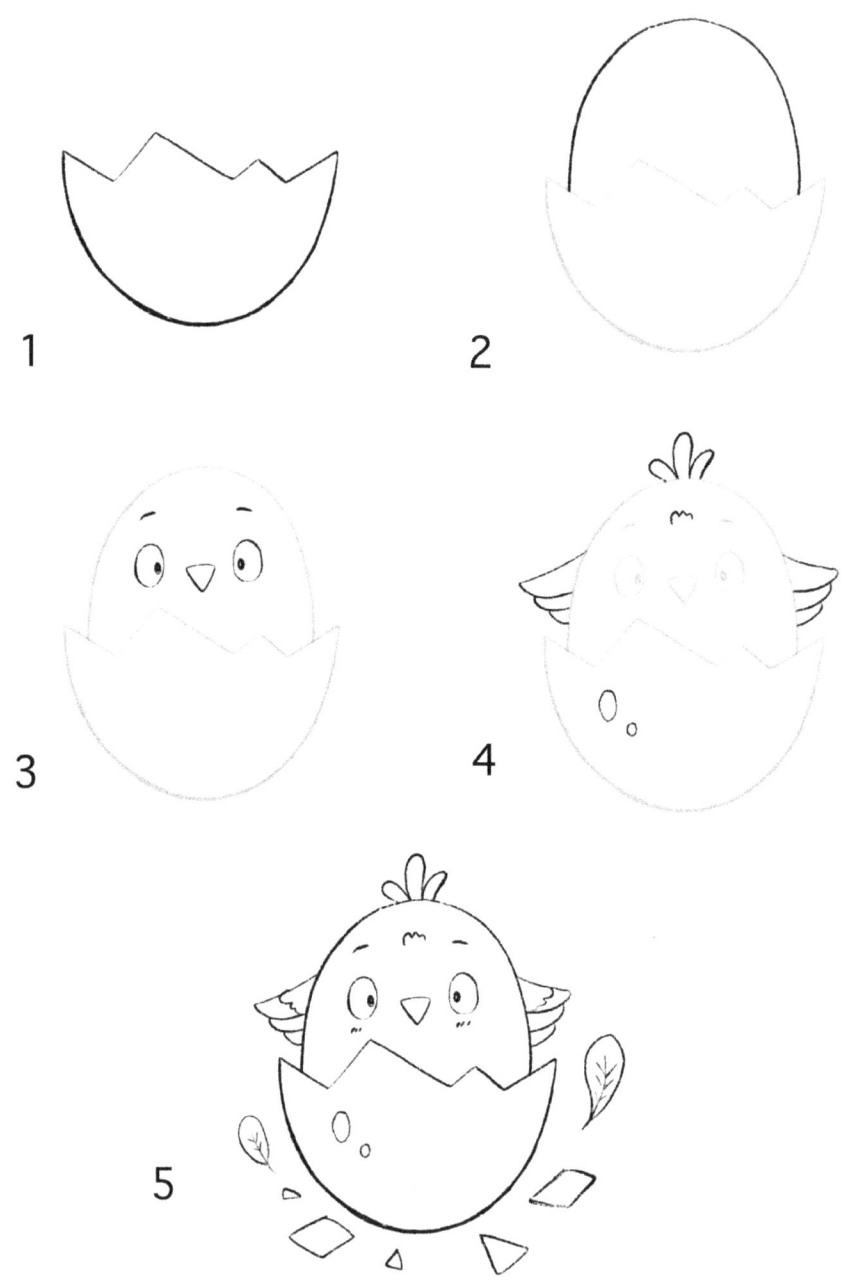

1

2

3

4

5

Practice here!

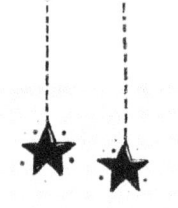

Cow

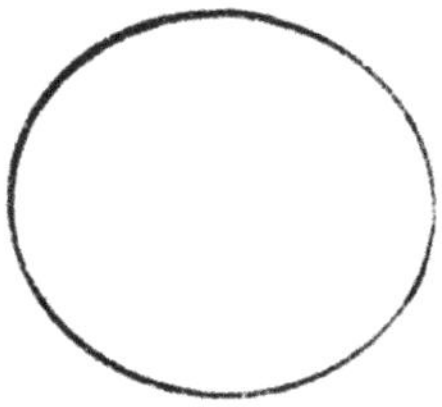

1

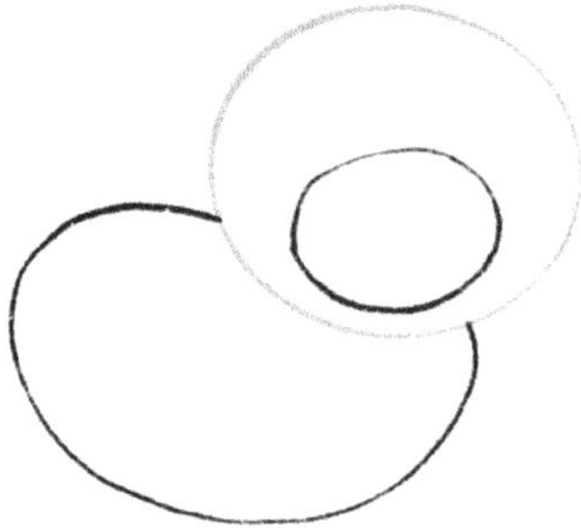

2

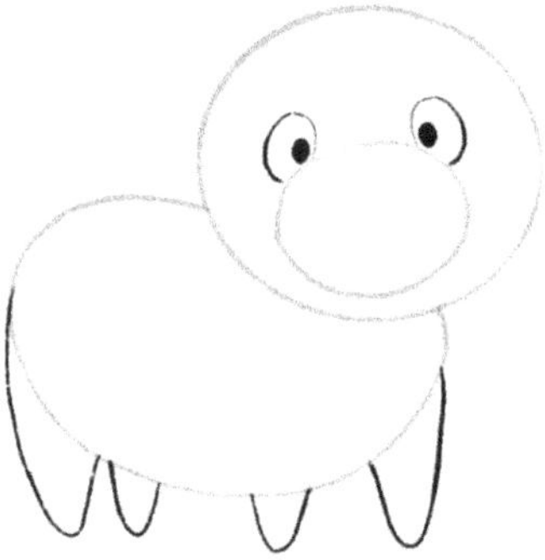

3

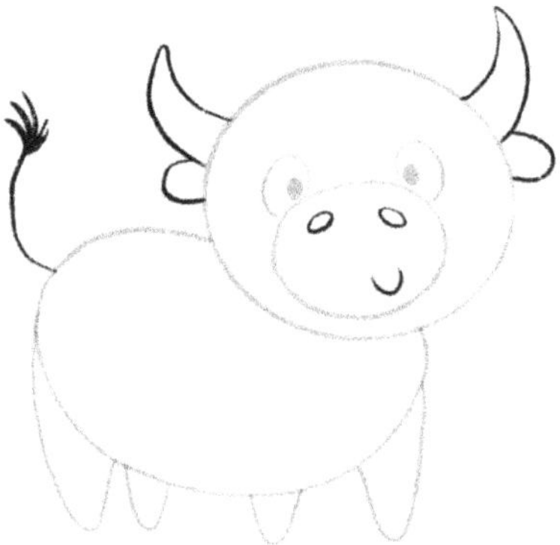

4

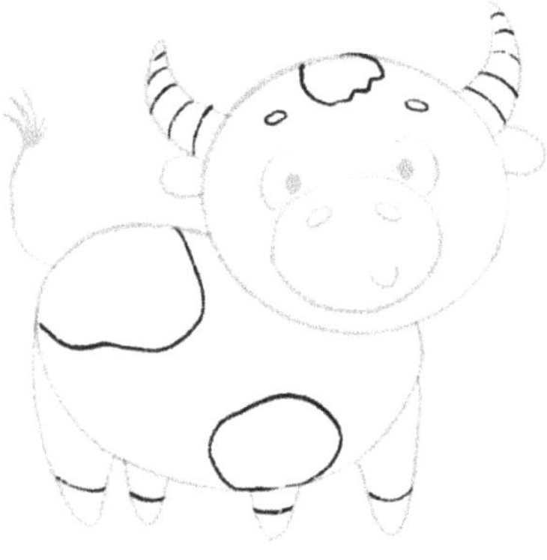

5

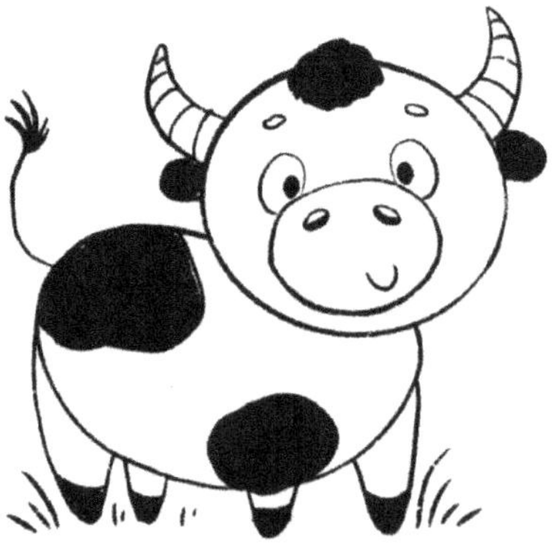

6

Practice here!

Crocodile

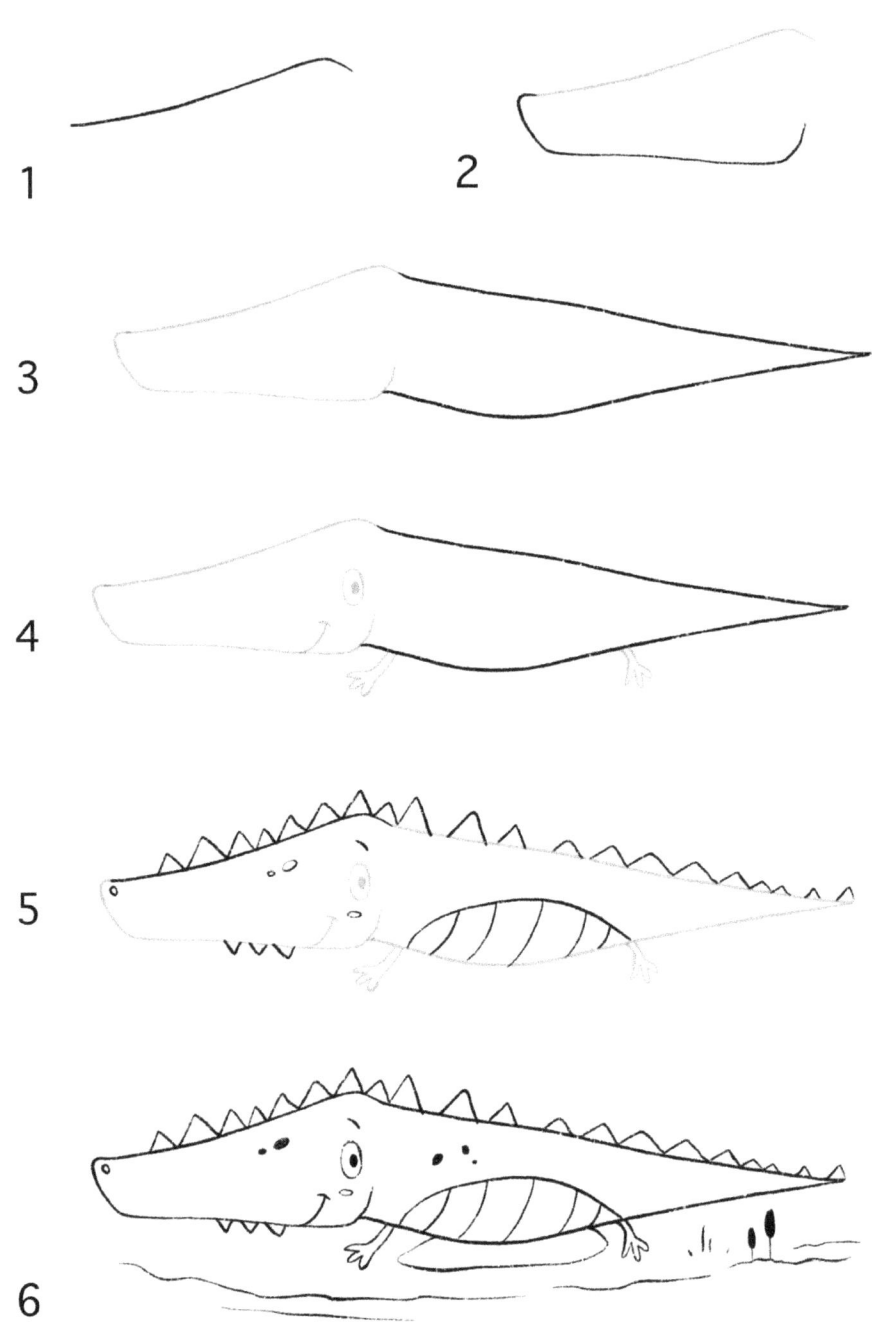

1

2

3

4

5

6

Practice here!

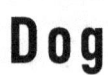

Dog

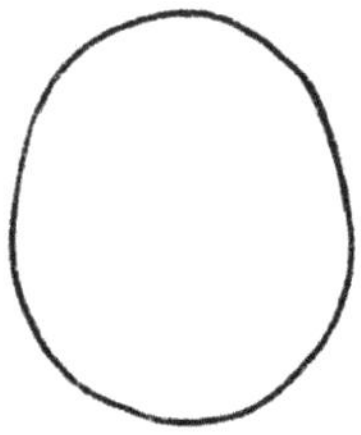

1

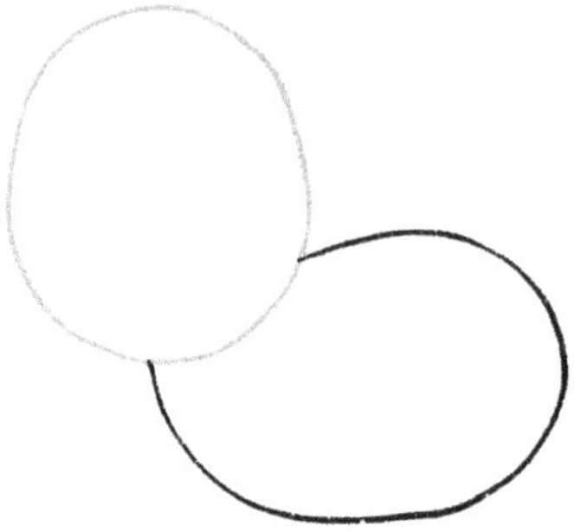

2

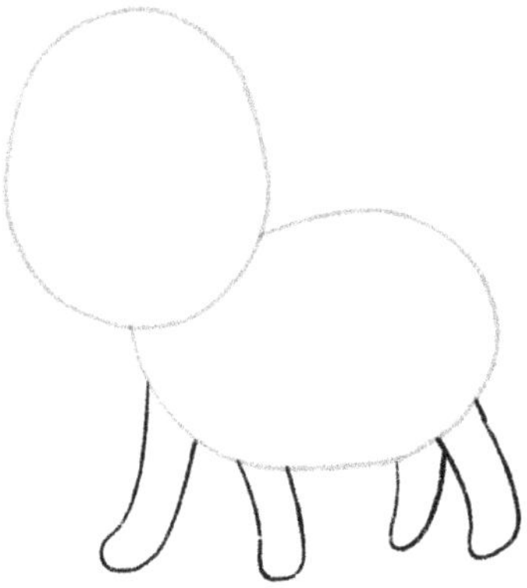

3

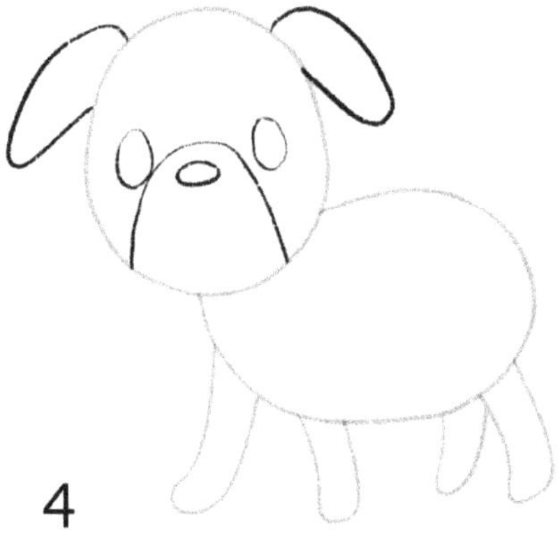

4

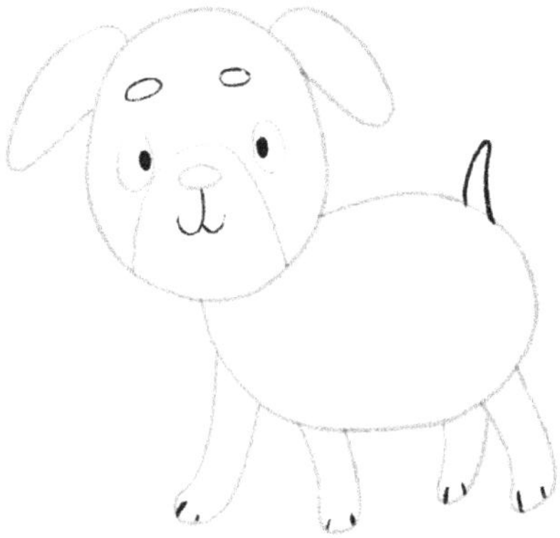

5

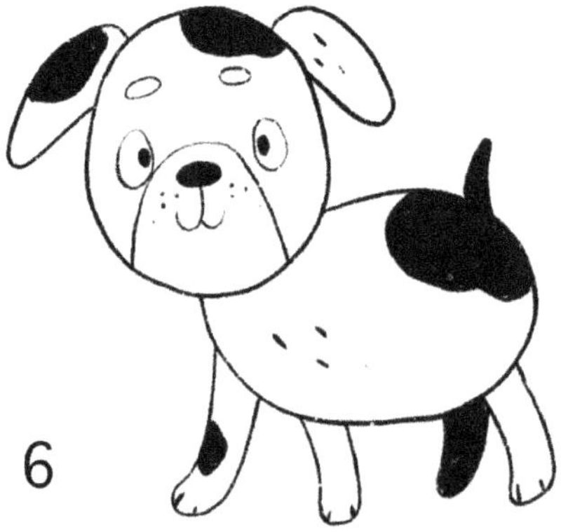

6

Practice here!

Give this little guy a house and some toys!

Dolphin

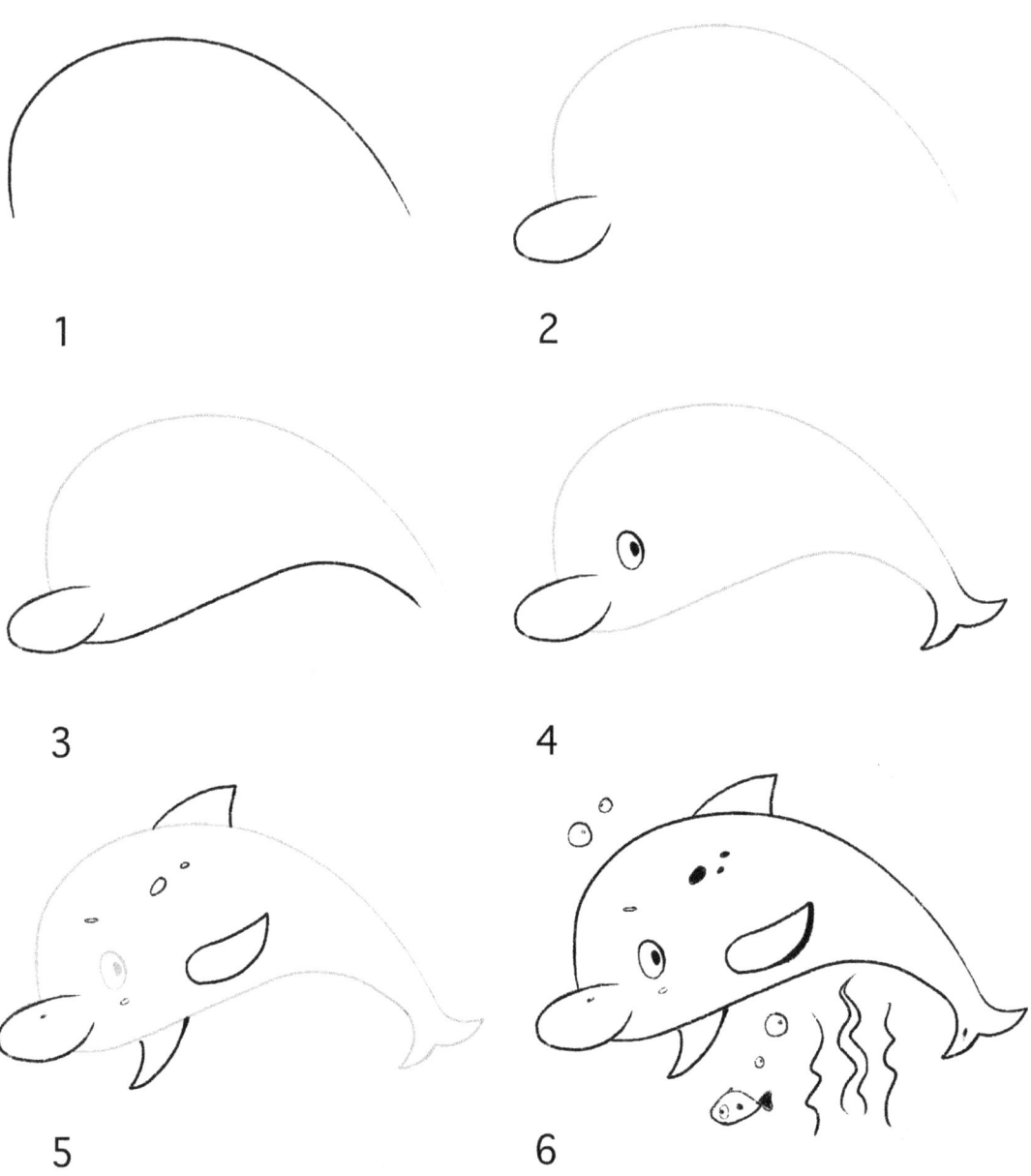

1

2

3

4

5

6

26

Practice here!

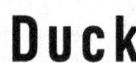

Duck

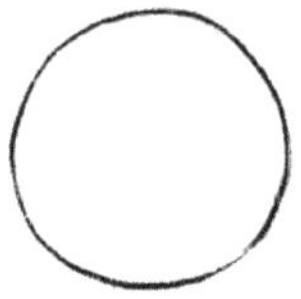

1

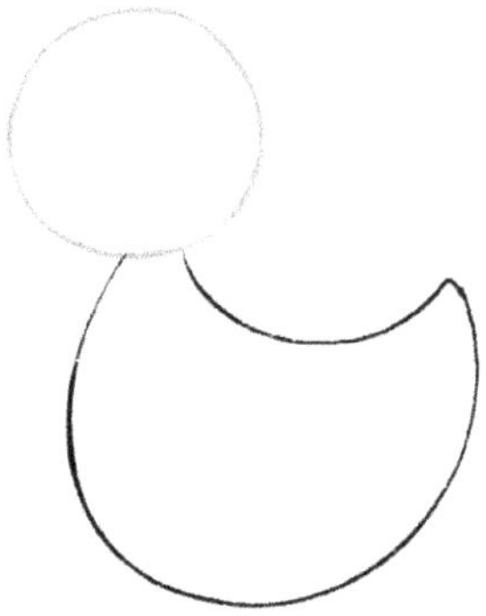

2

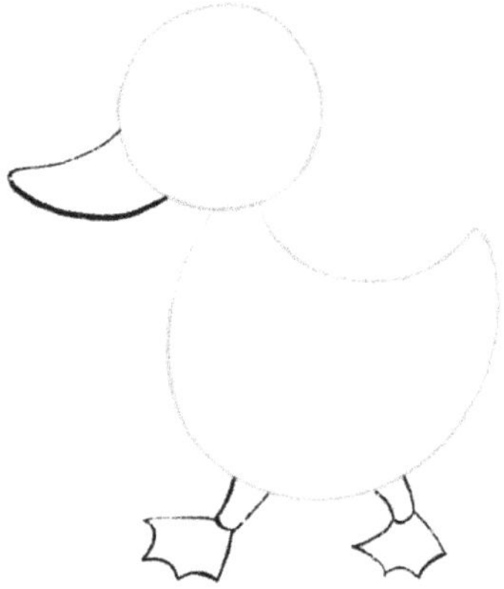

3

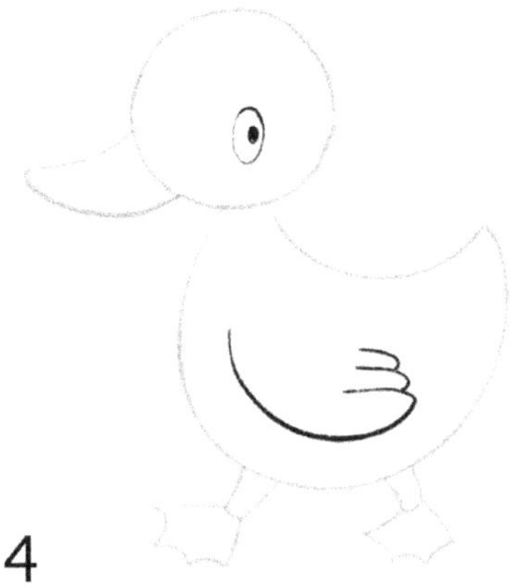

4

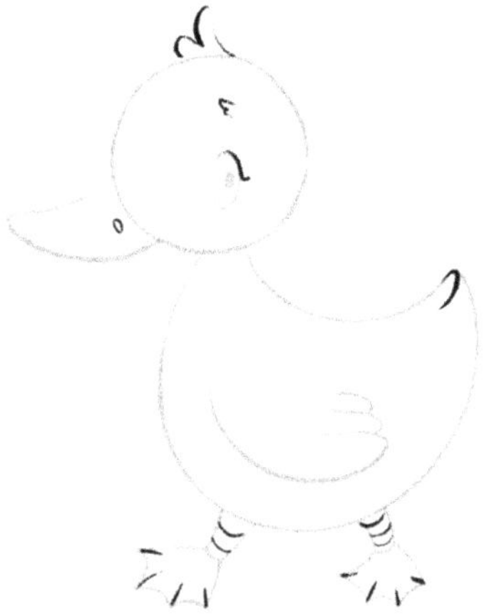

5

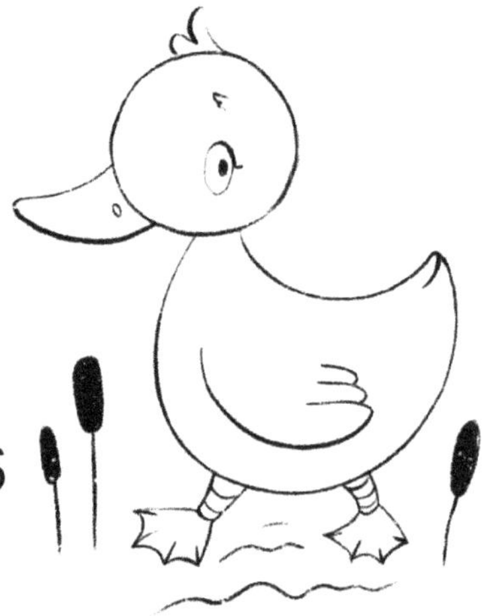

6

Practice here!

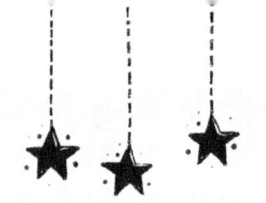

Elephant

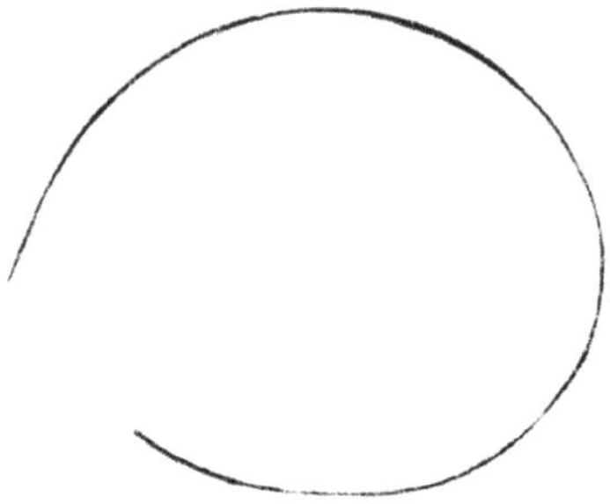

1

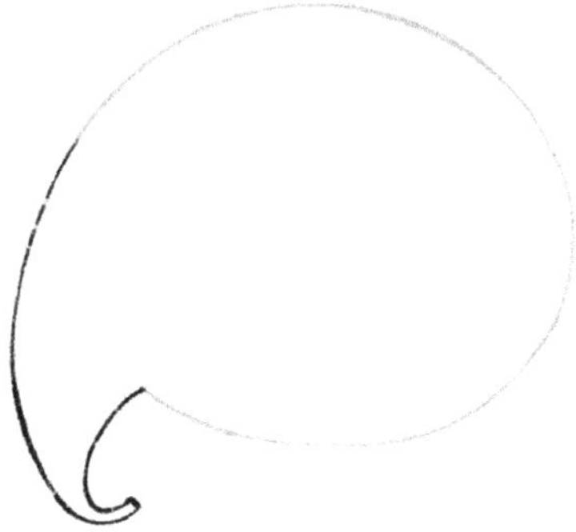

2

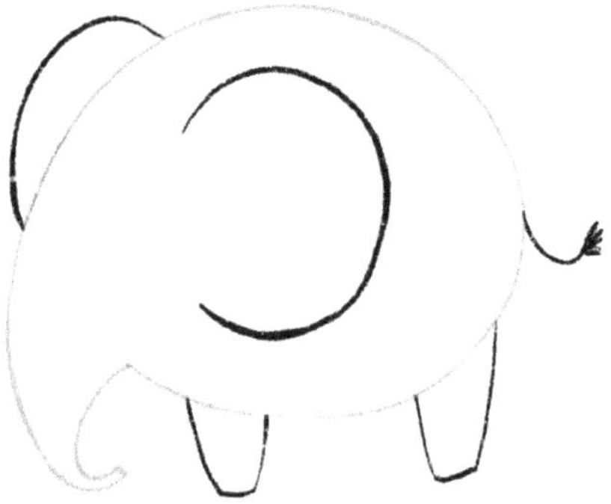

3

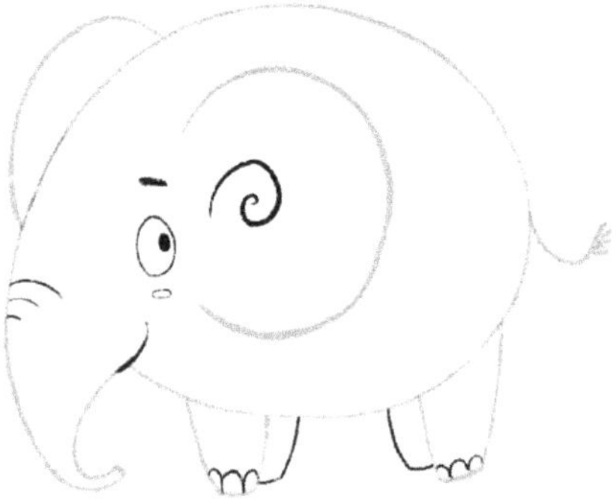

4

5

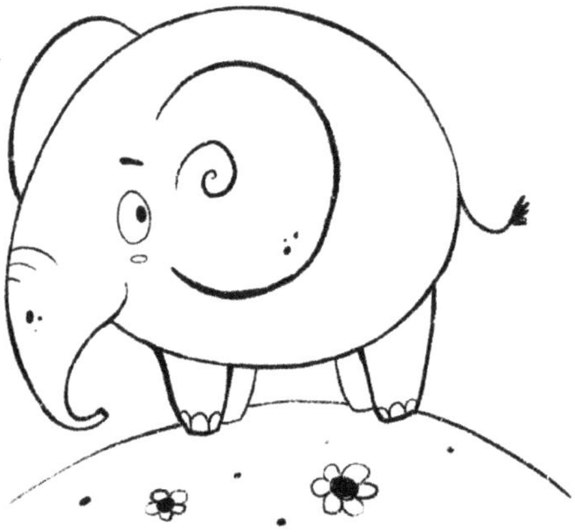

Practice here!

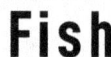

Fish

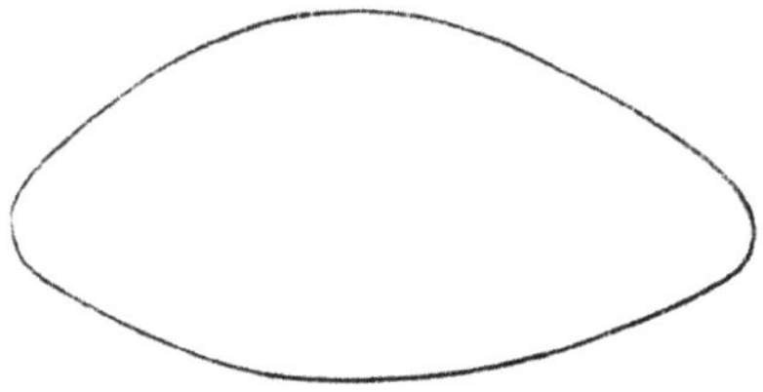

1

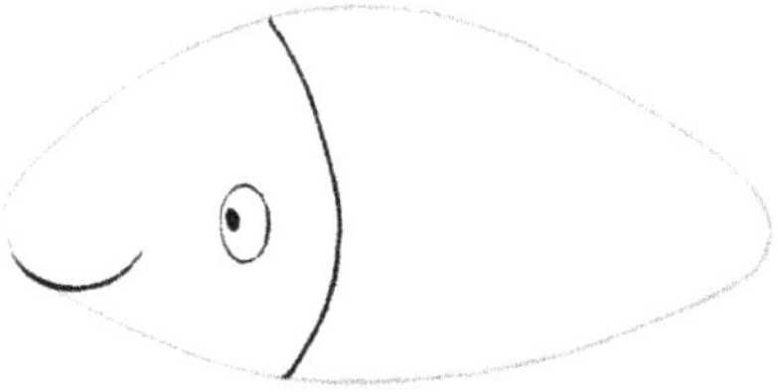

2

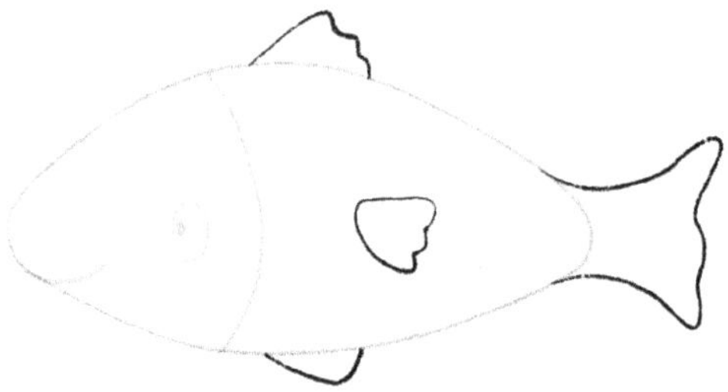

3

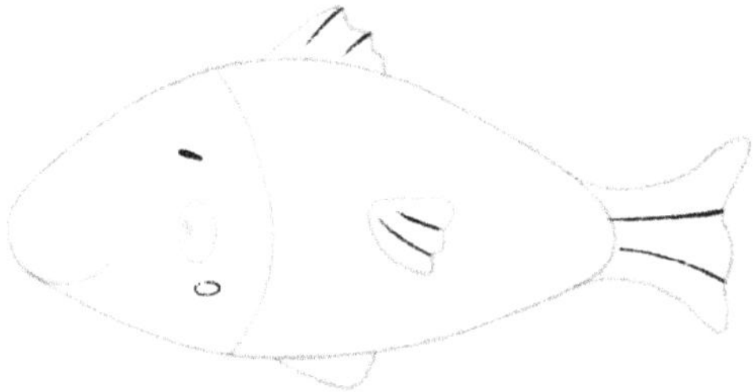

4

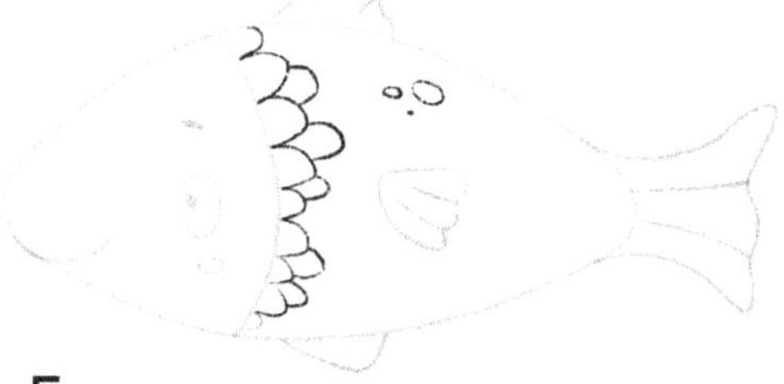

5

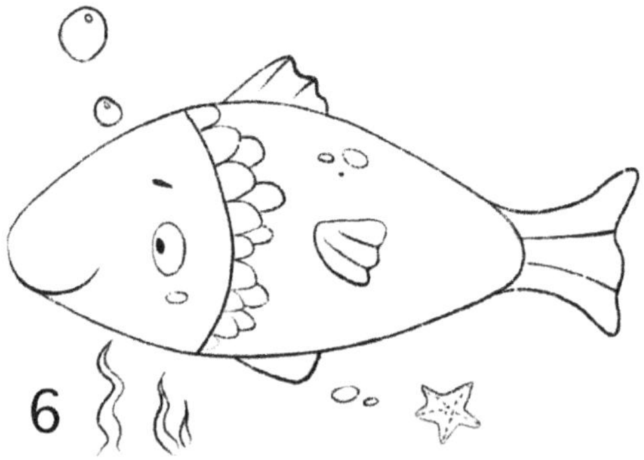

6

Practice here!

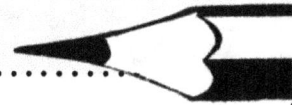

Try to draw a very fat fish or a reeeally skinny one!

Flamingo

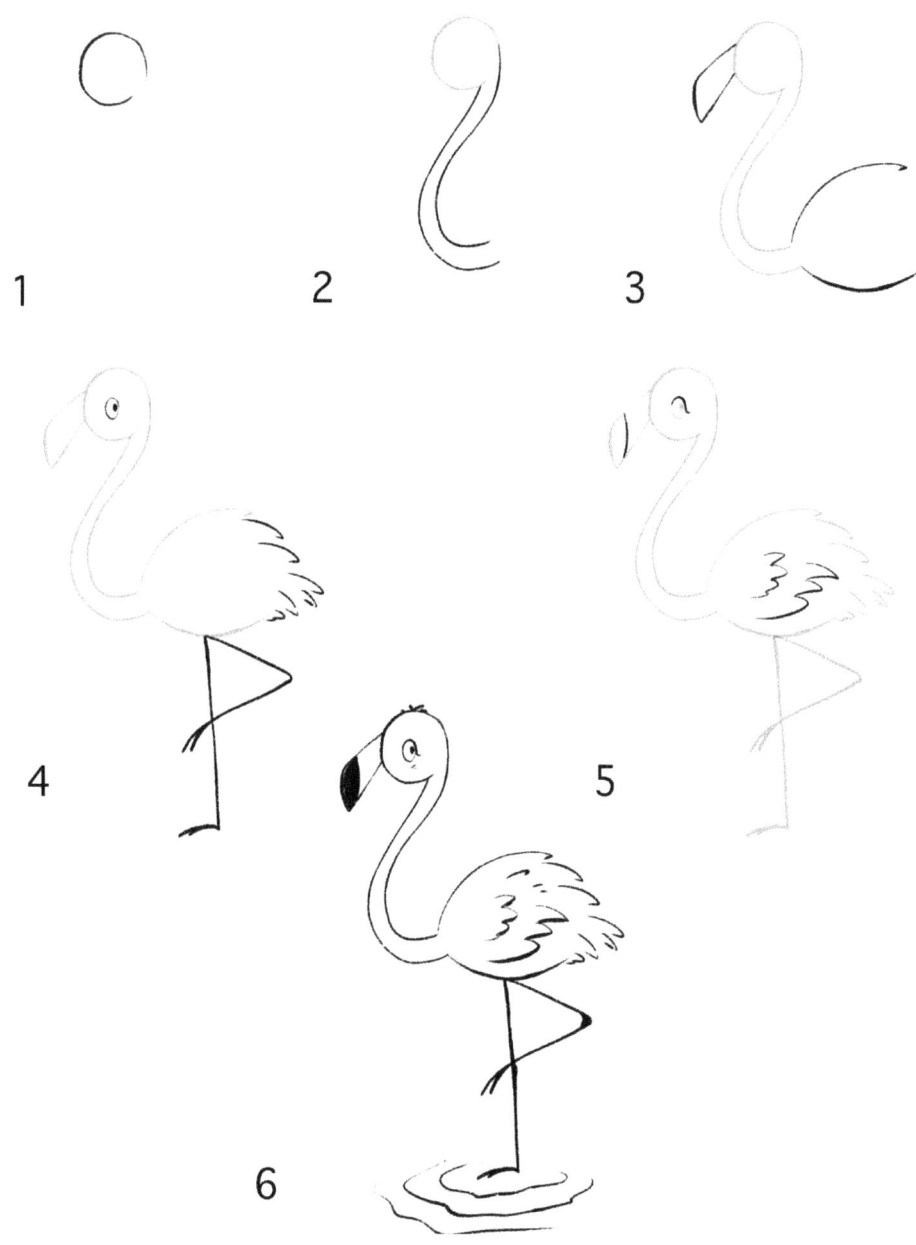

1

2

3

4

5

6

Practice here!

Fox

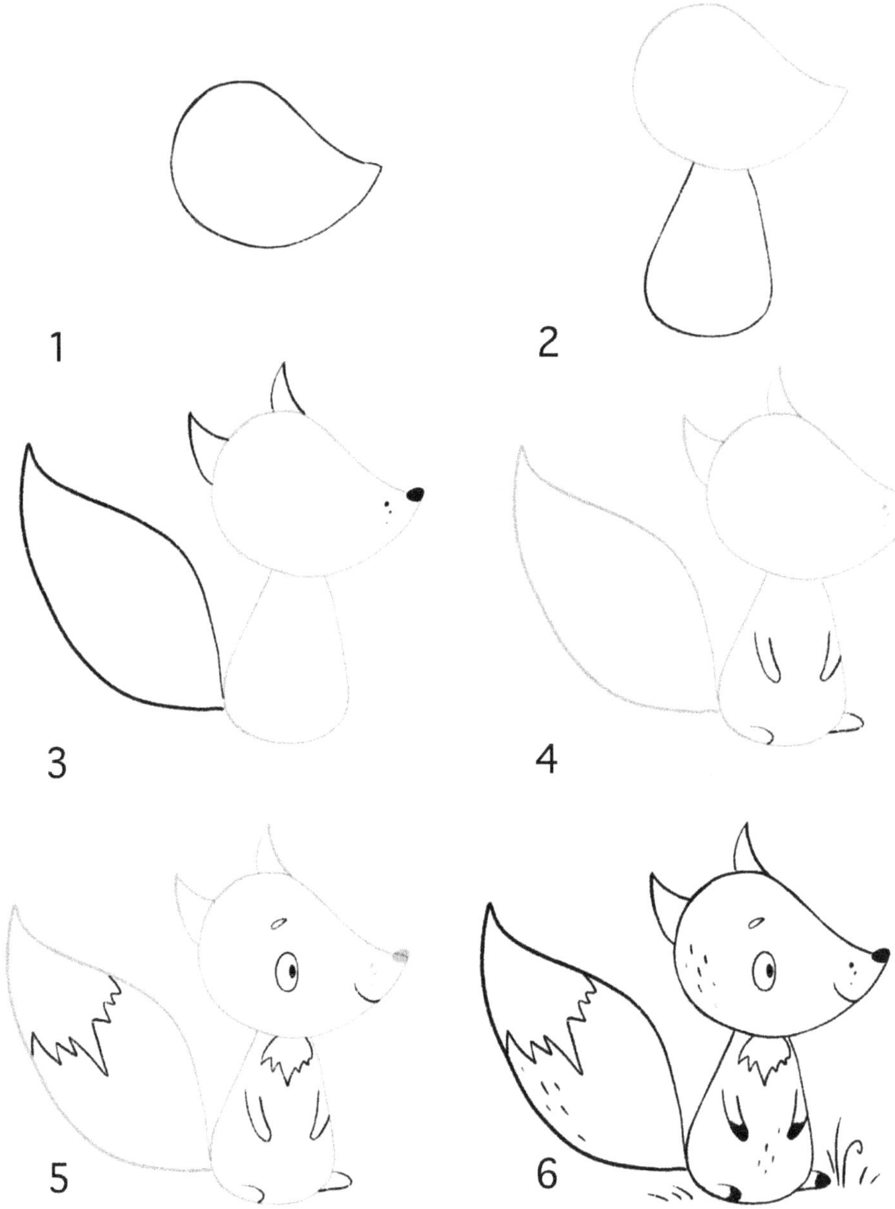

1

2

3

4

5

6

Practice here!

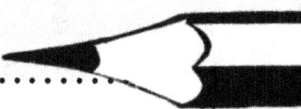

Frog

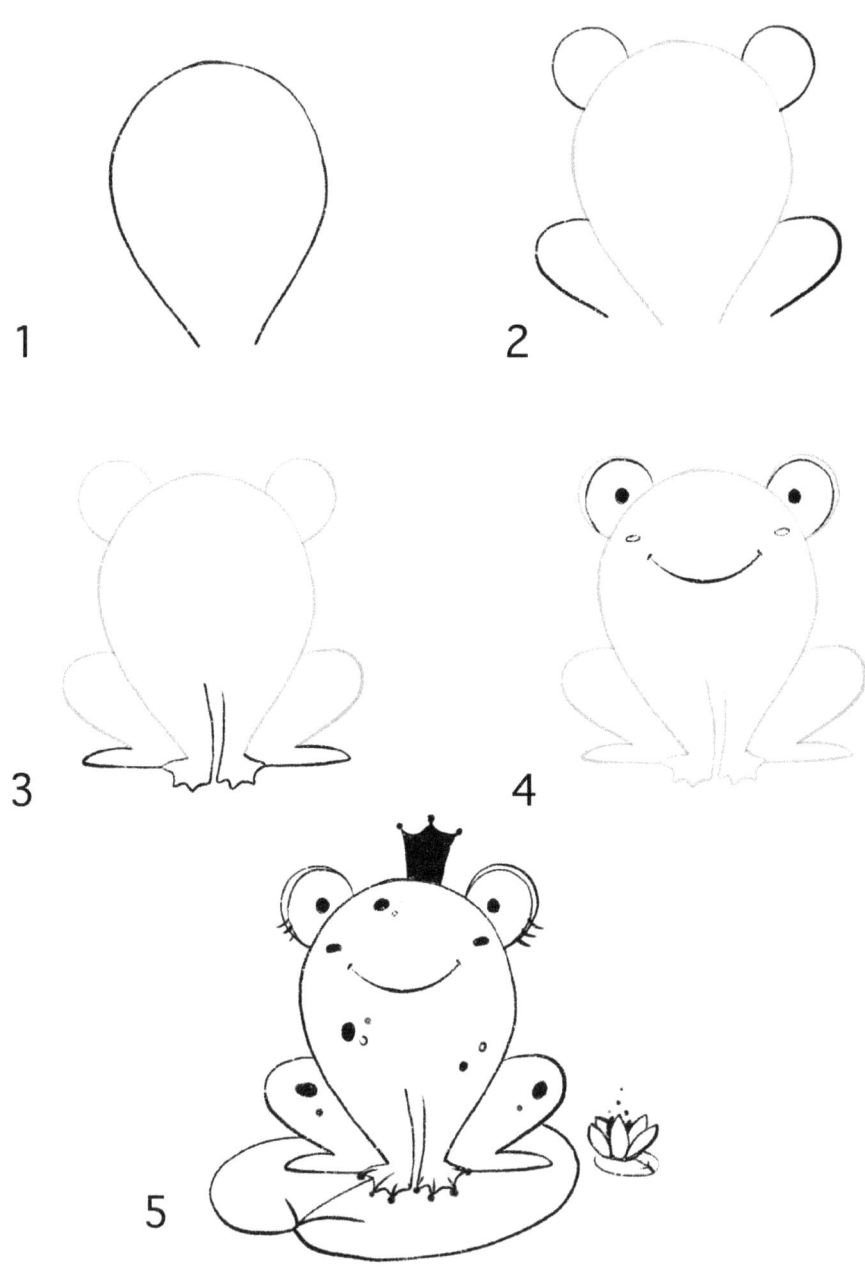

1

2

3

4

5

Practice here!

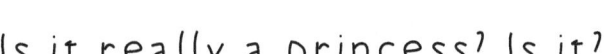

Is it really a princess? Is it?

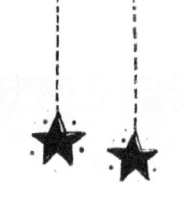

Giraffe

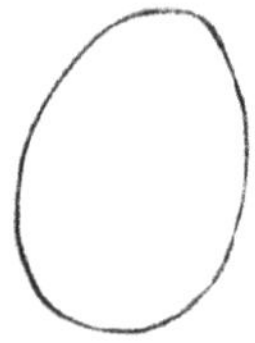

1

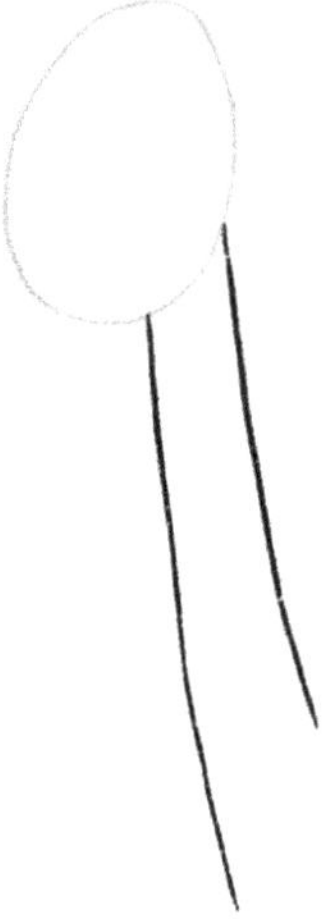

2

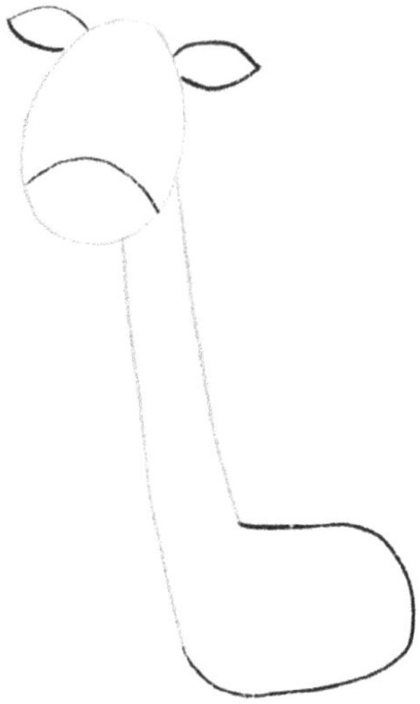

3

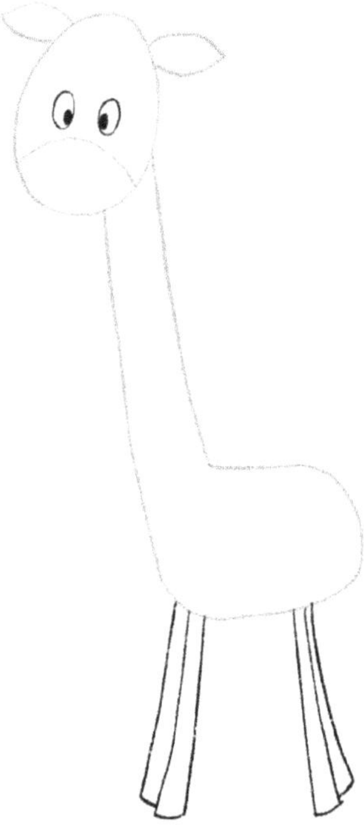

4

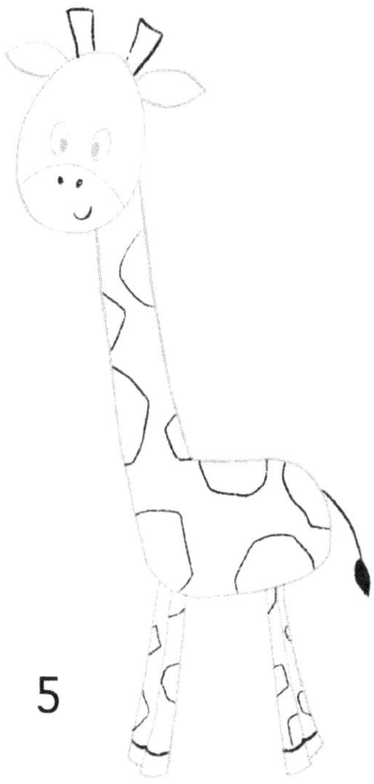

5

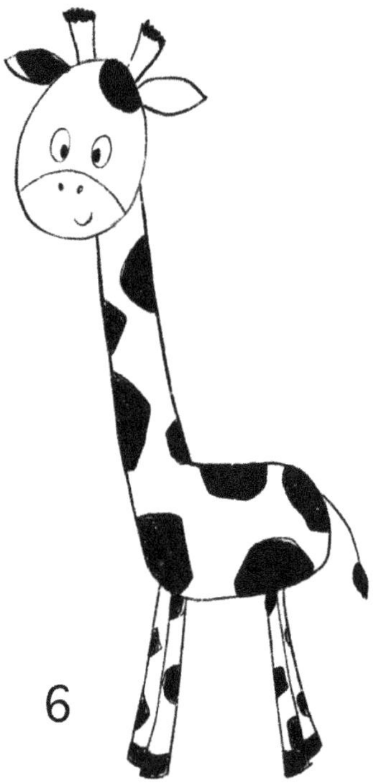

6

Practice here!

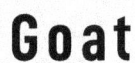

Goat

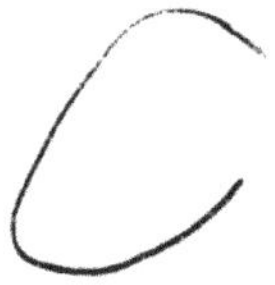

1

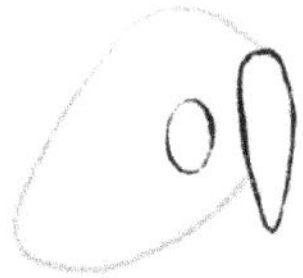

2

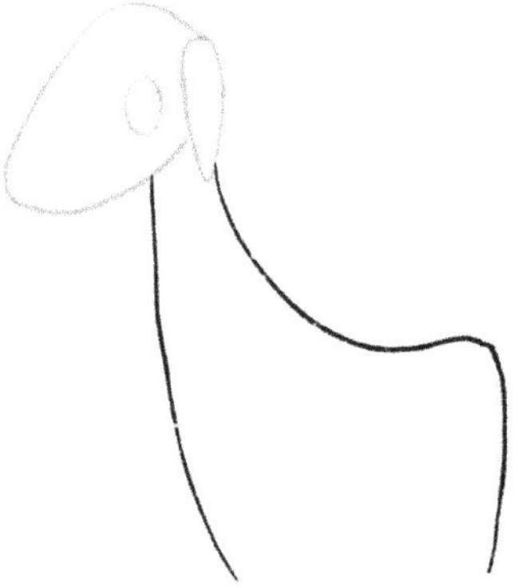

3

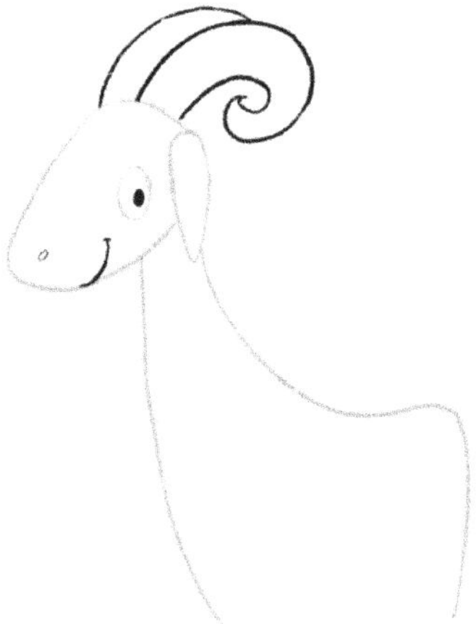

4

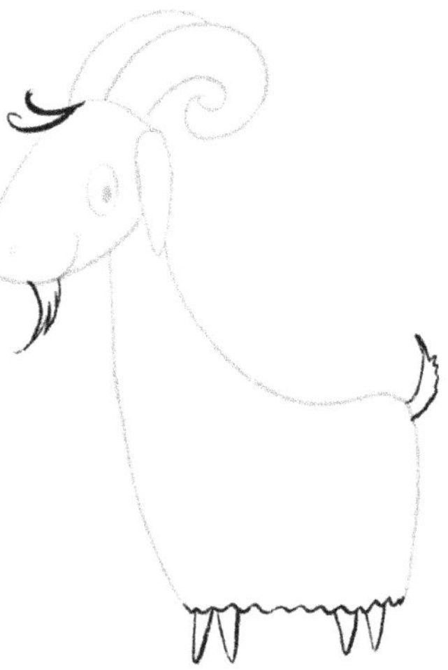

5

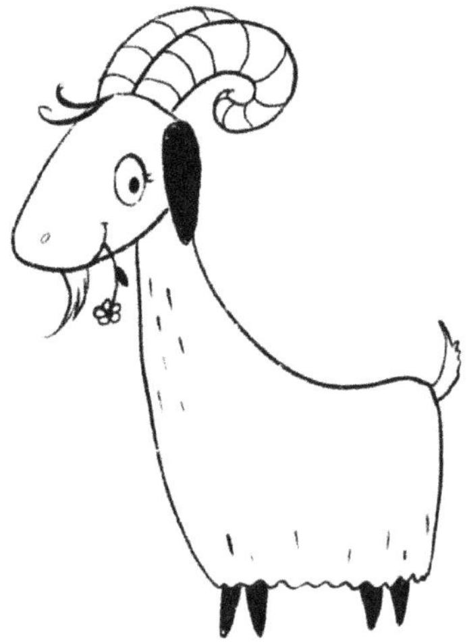

6

Practice here!

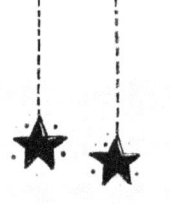

Hamster

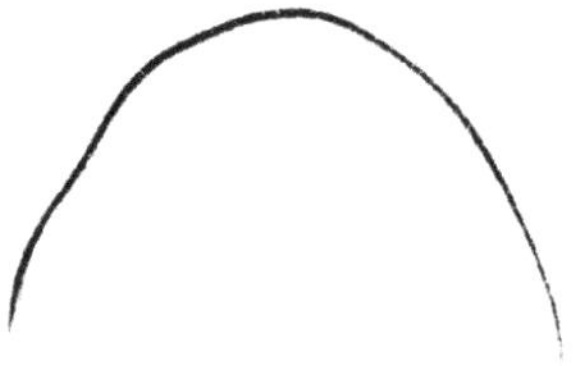

1

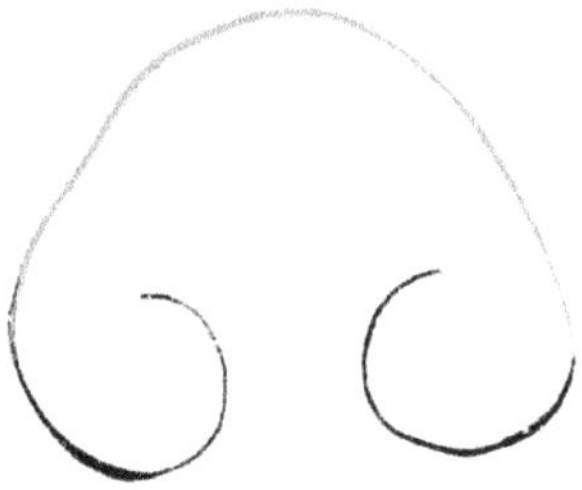

2

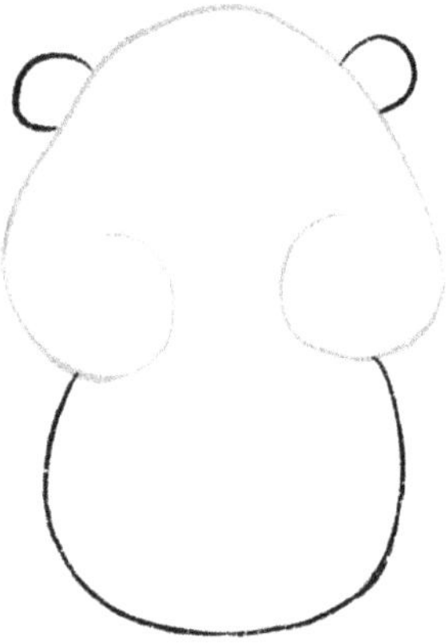

3

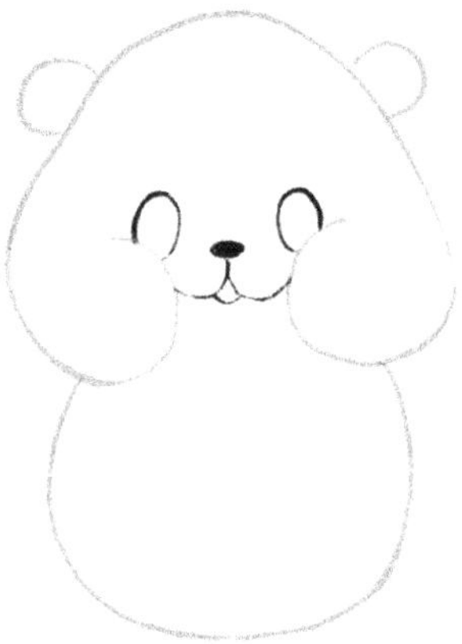

4

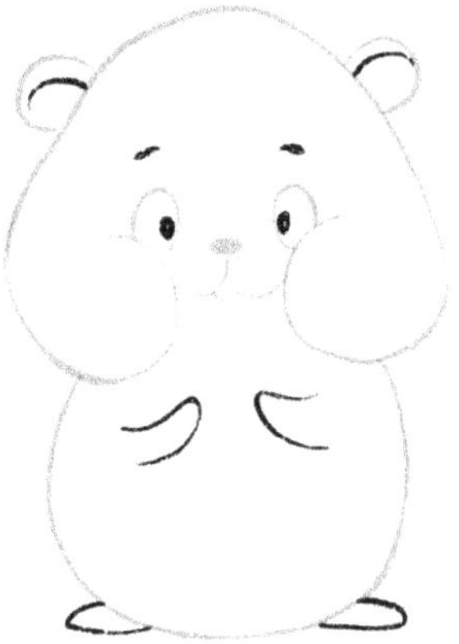

5

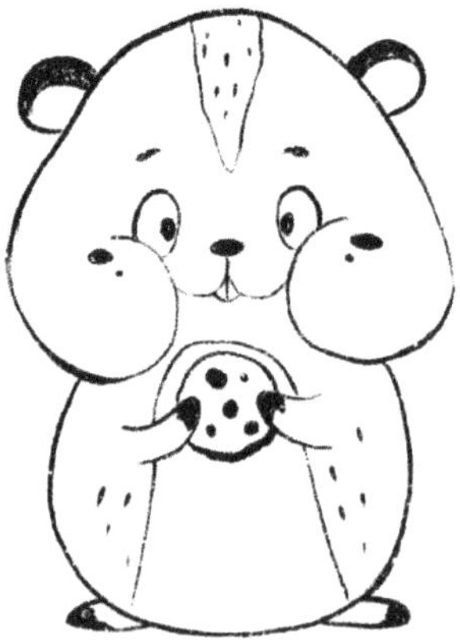

6

44

Practice here!

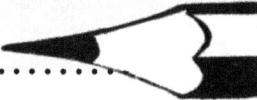

Cookies are very bad for hamsters, better give him some vegetables!

Hedgehog

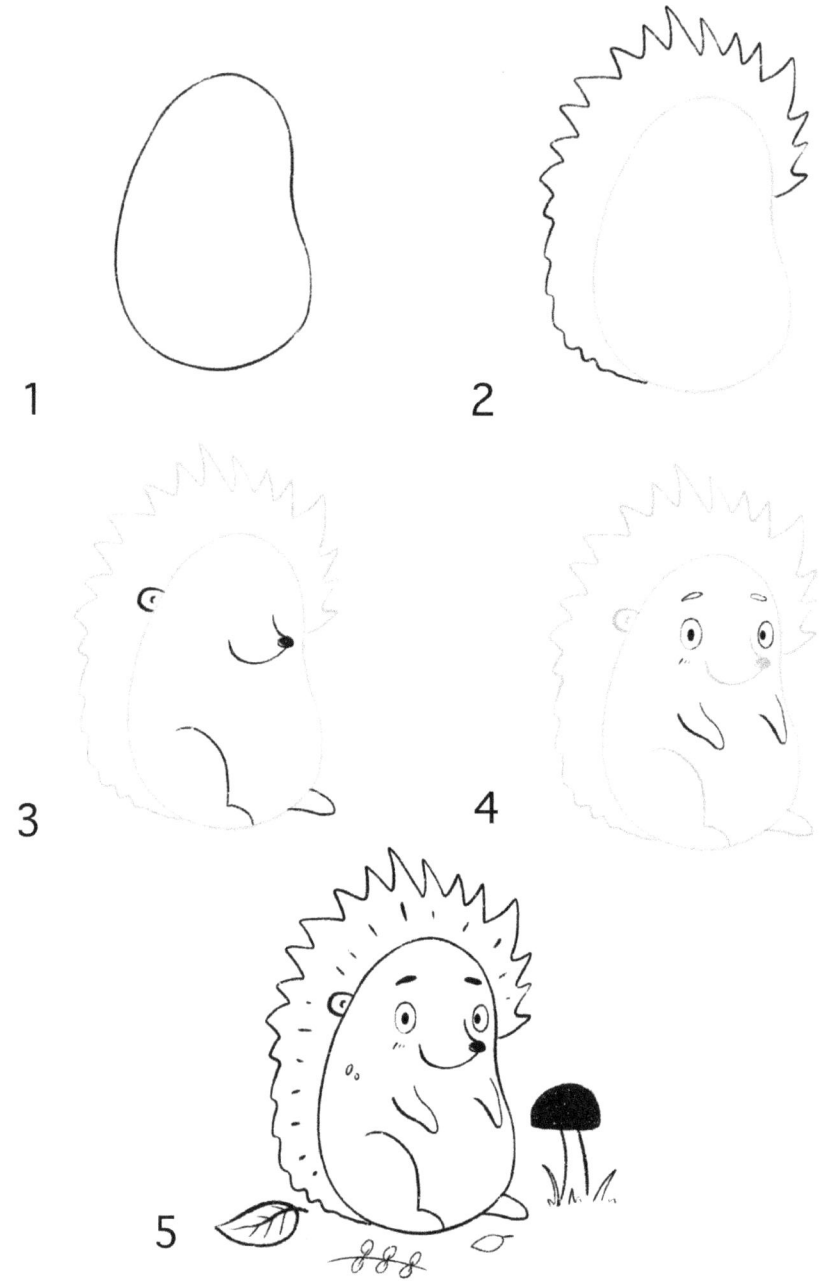

1

2

3

4

5

Practice here!

Hippo

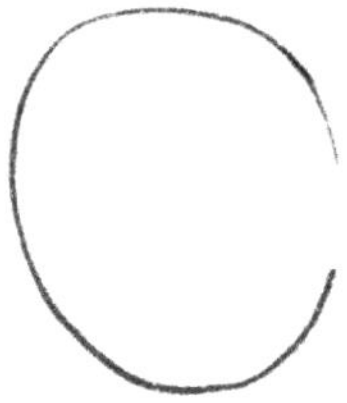

1

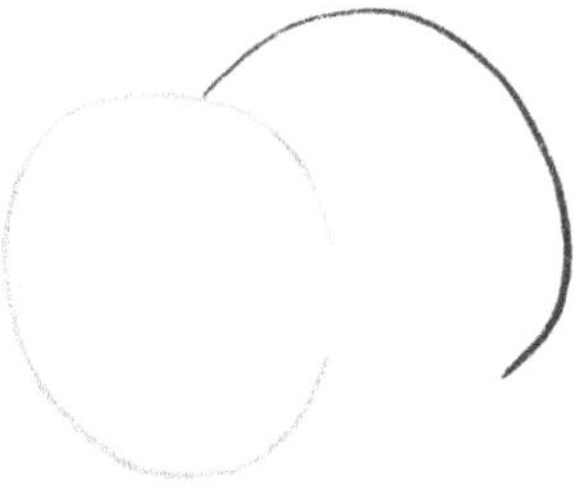

2

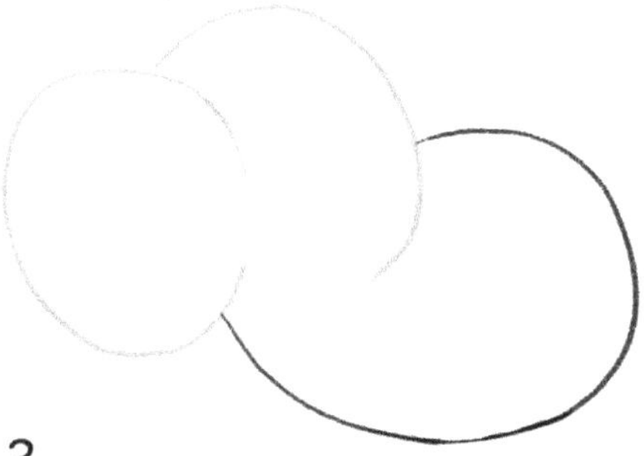

3

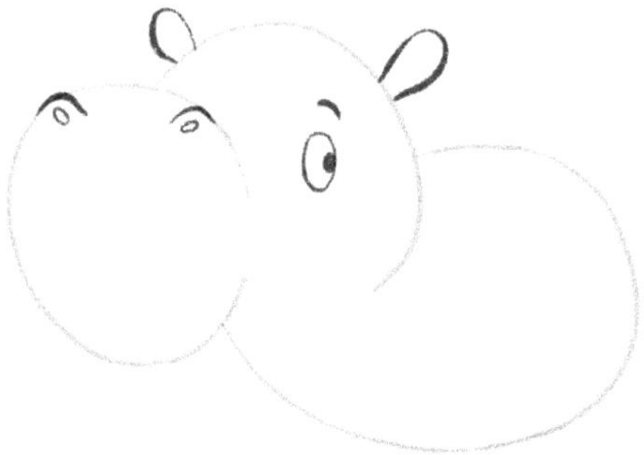

4

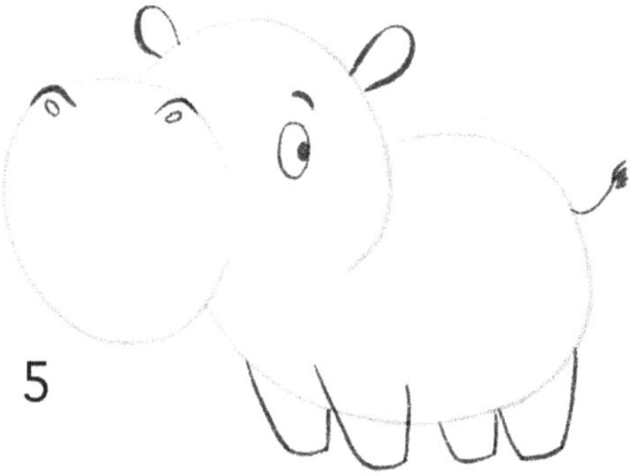

5

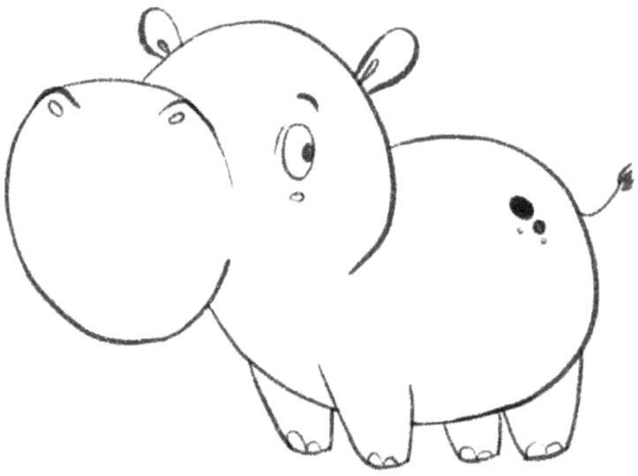

6

Practice here!

Horse

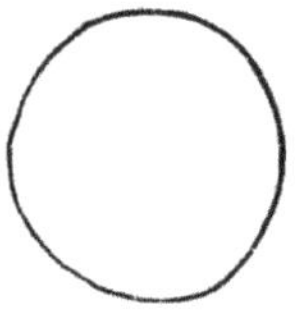

1

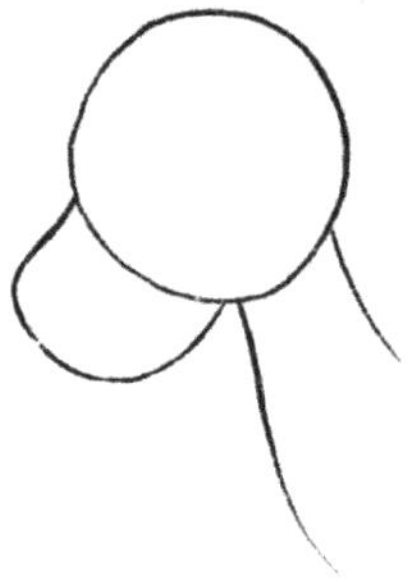

2

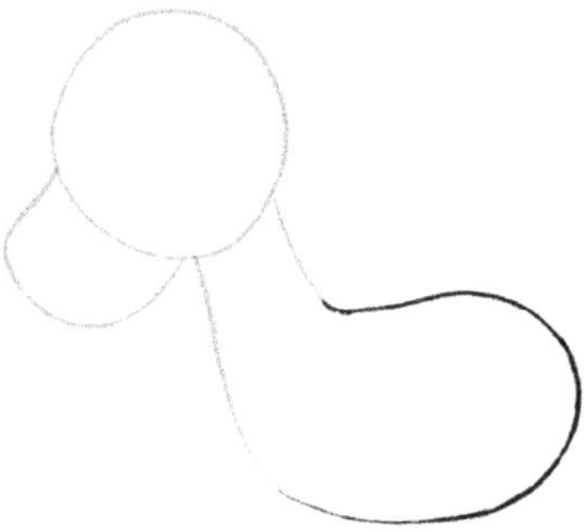

3

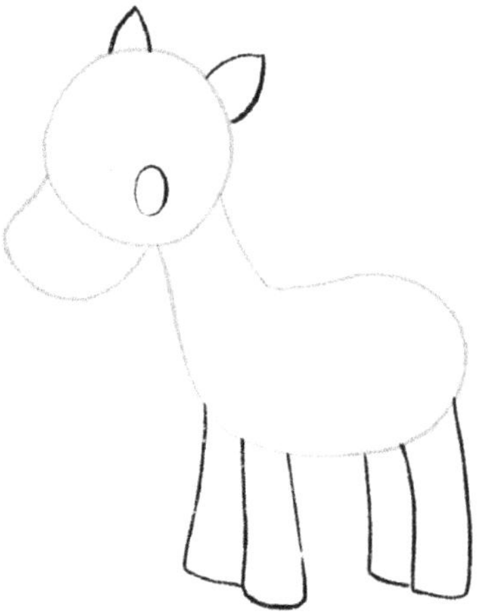

4

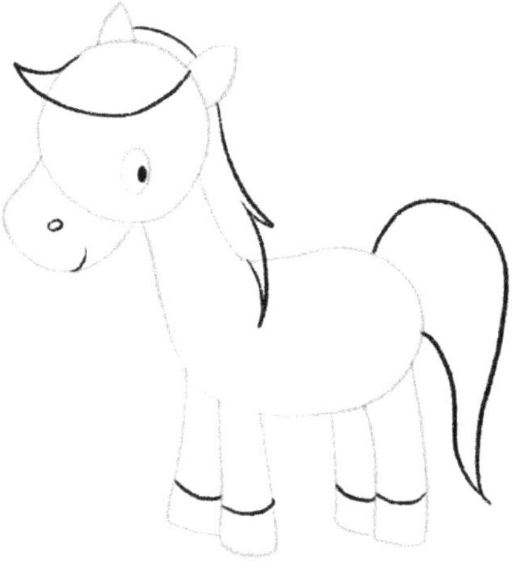

5

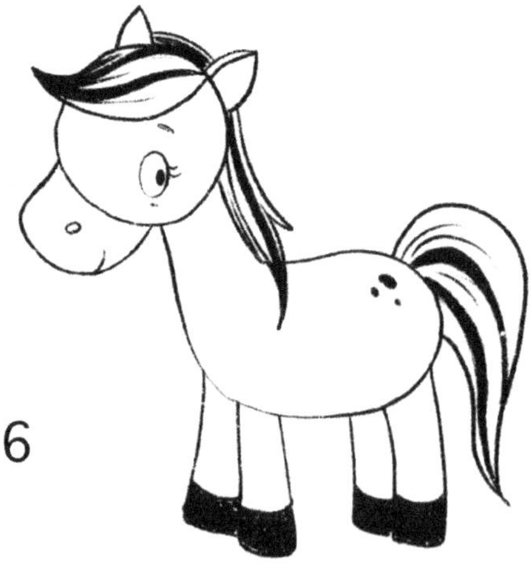

6

Practice here!

Horse is one of the most difficult animals to draw, give it a time!

Kangaroo

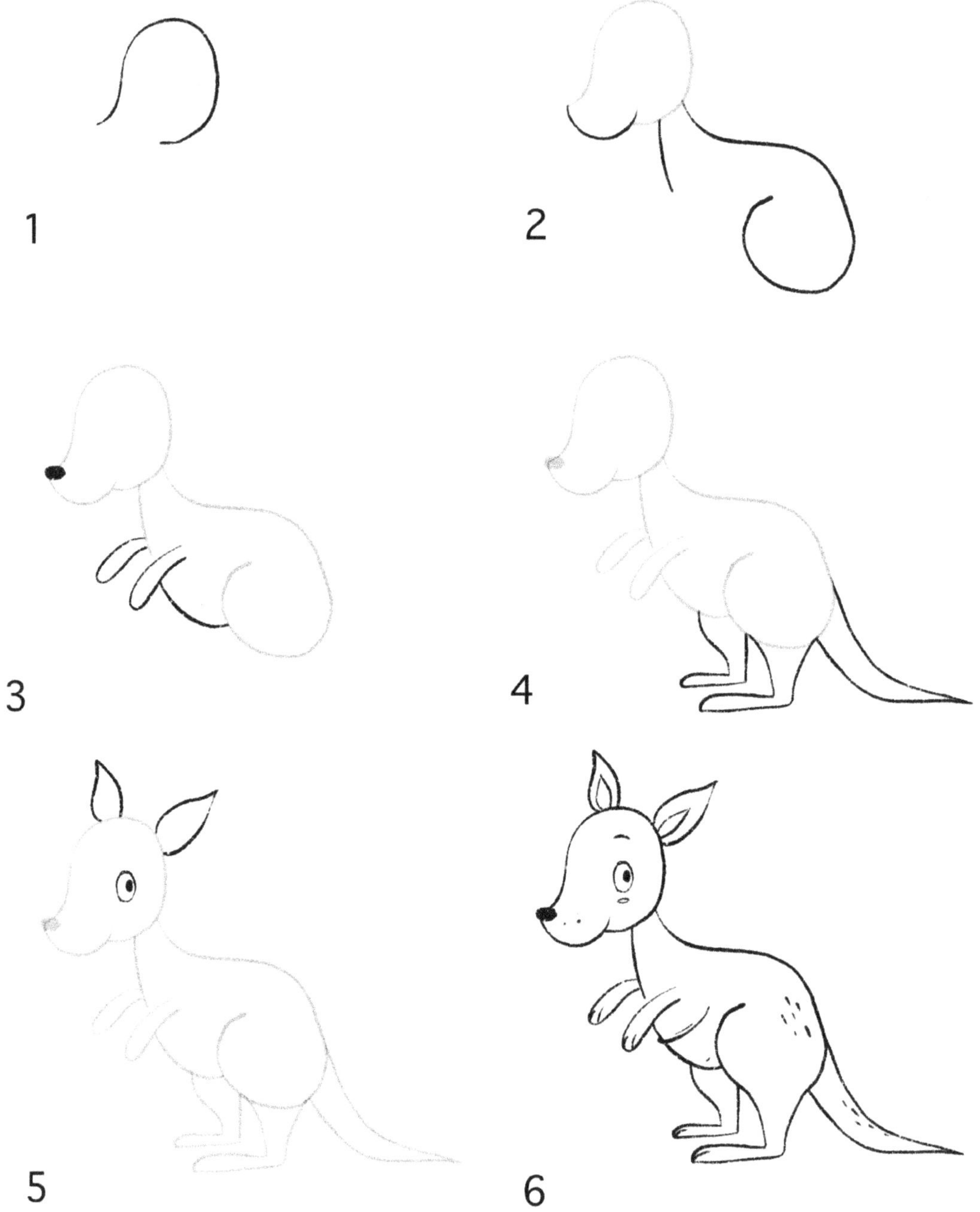

1

2

3

4

5

6

Practice here!

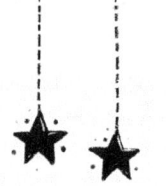

Kiwi

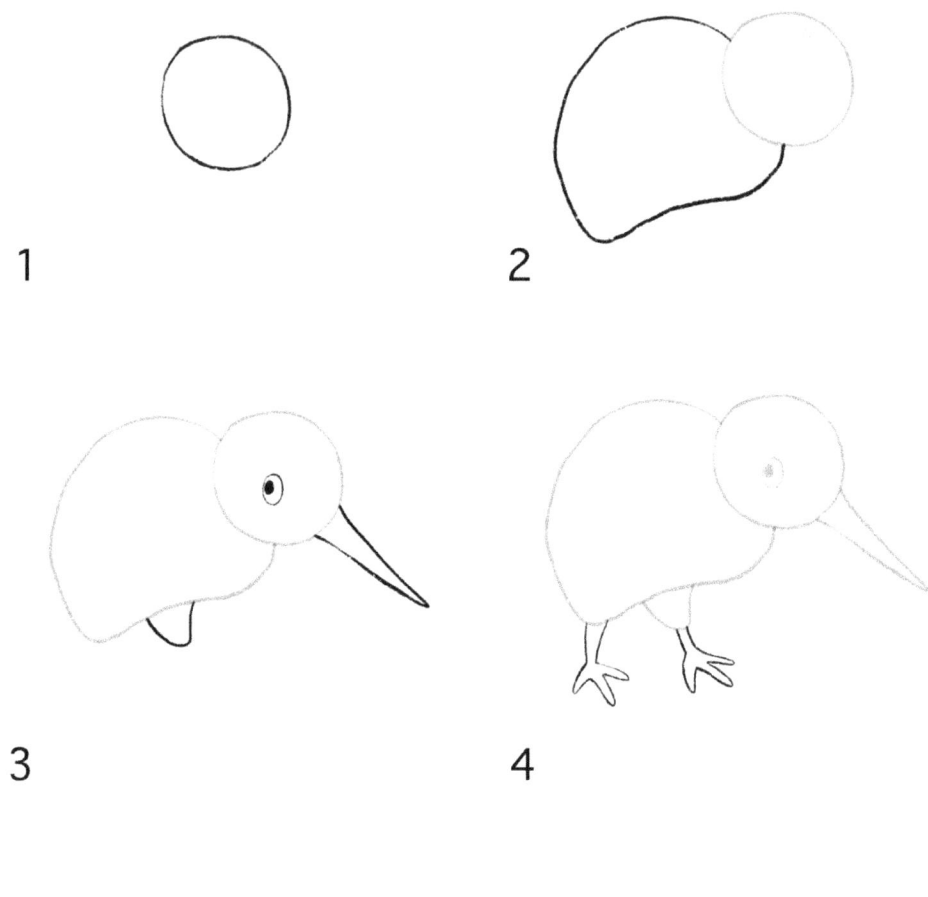

1

2

3

4

5

Practice here!

Did you know there were giant kiwis many many years ago??

Ladybug

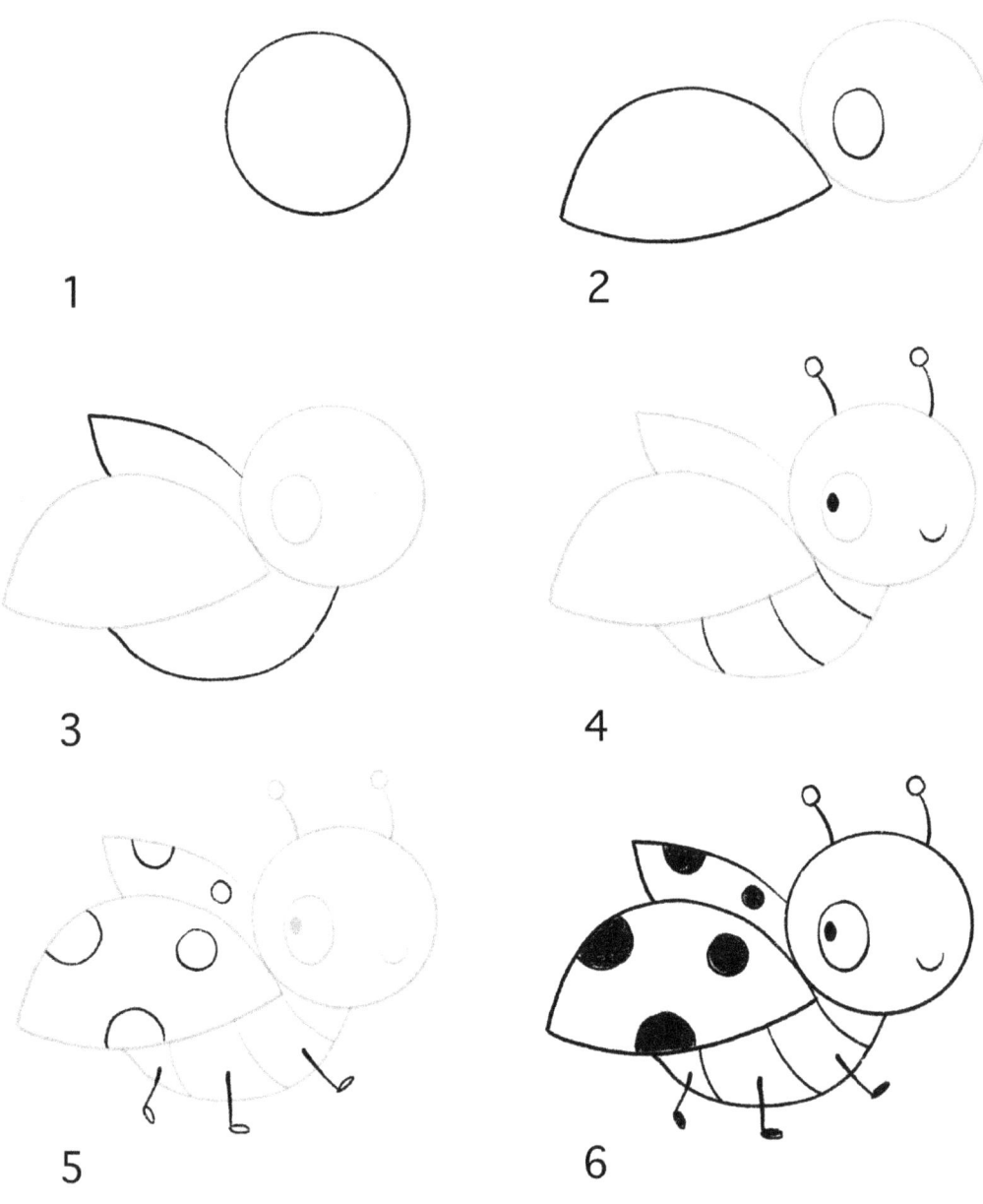

1

2

3

4

5

6

Practice here!

Lion

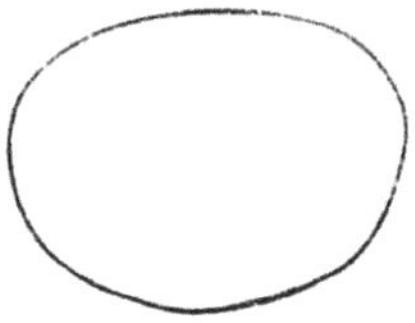

1

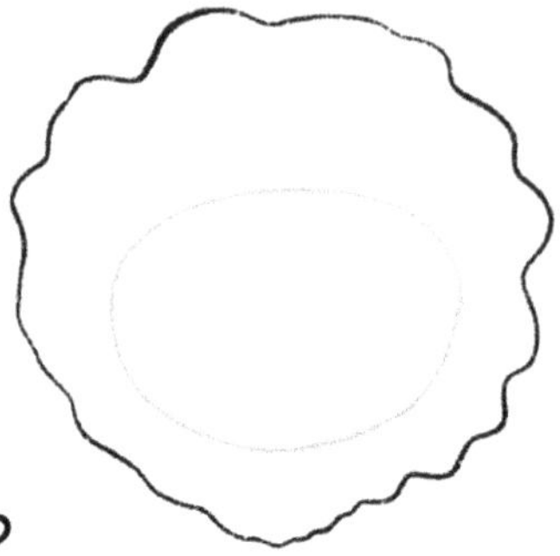

2

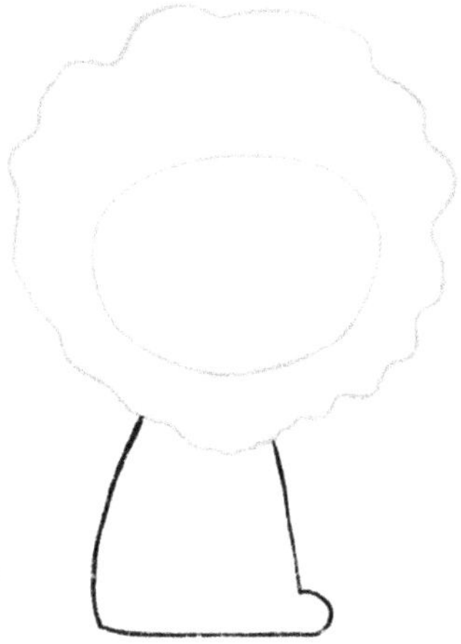

3

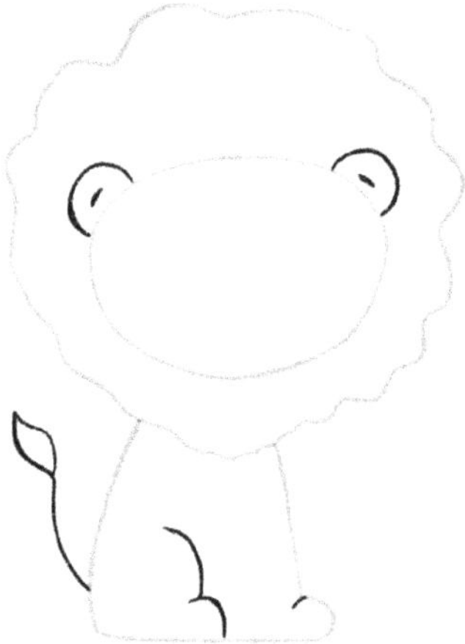

4

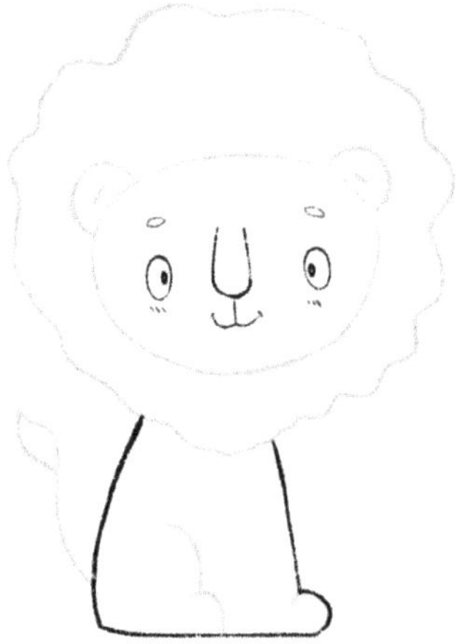

5

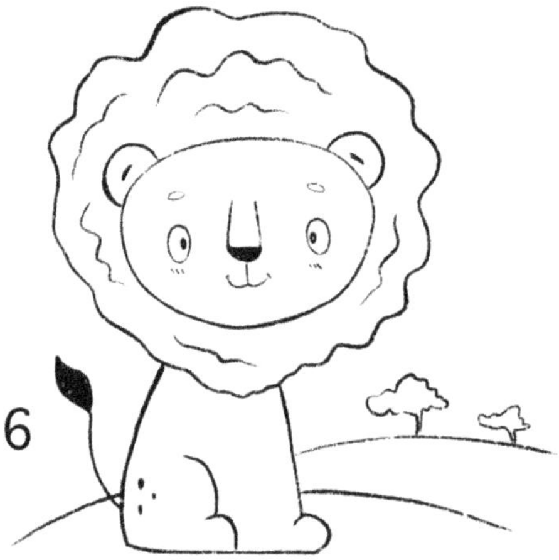

6

Practice here!

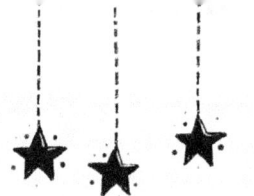

Llama

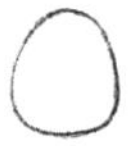

1

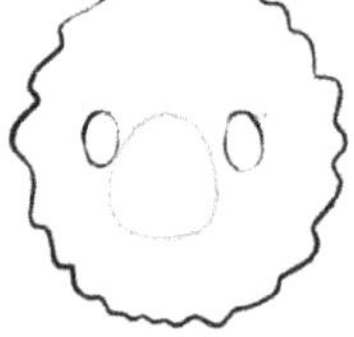

2

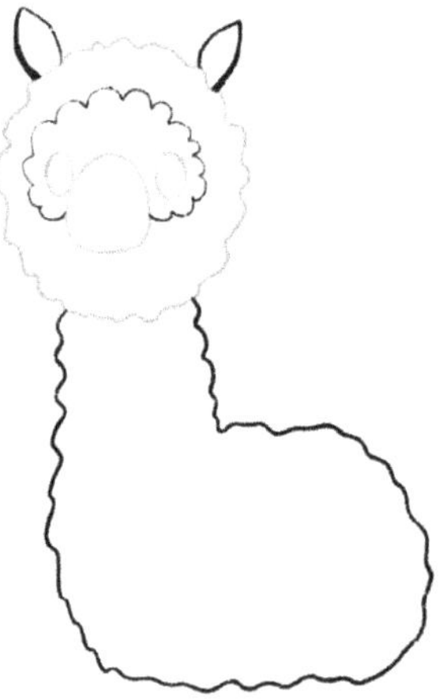

3

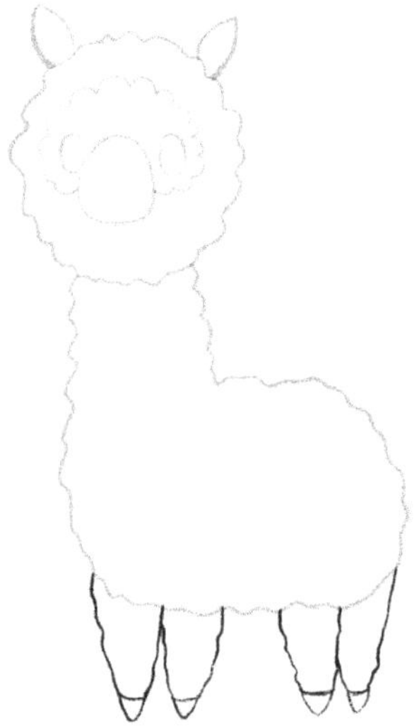

4

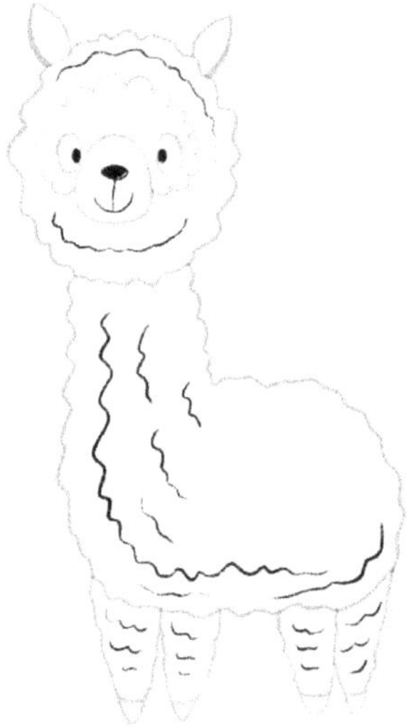

5

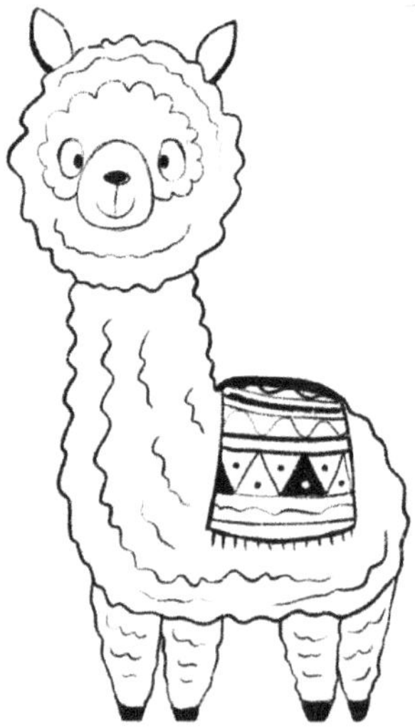

6

Practice here!

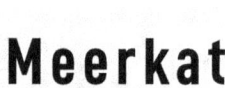

Meerkat

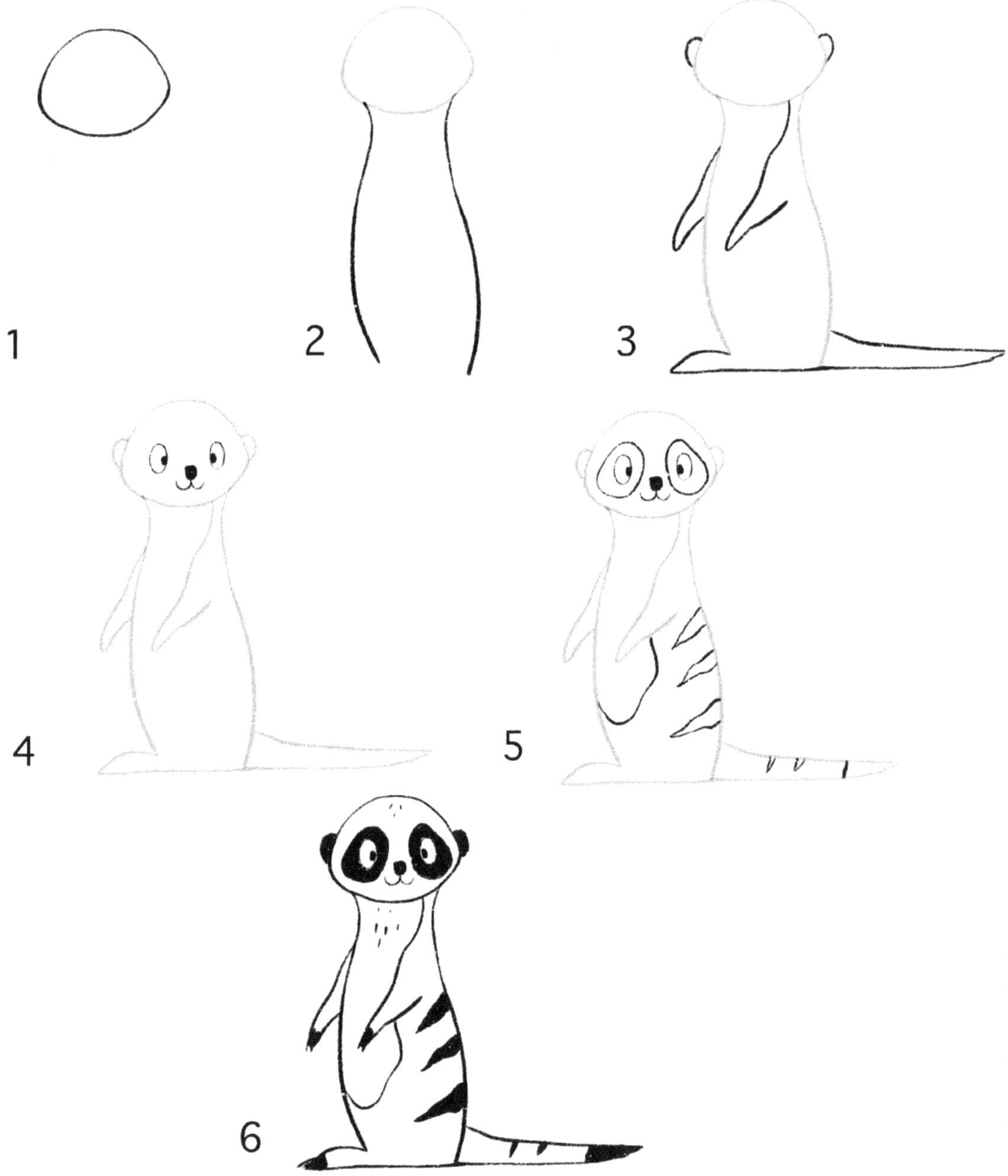

1

2

3

4

5

6

62

Practice here!

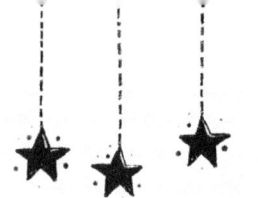

Monkey

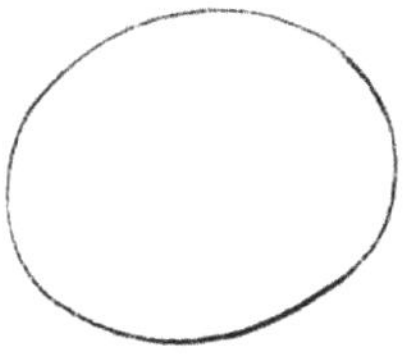

1

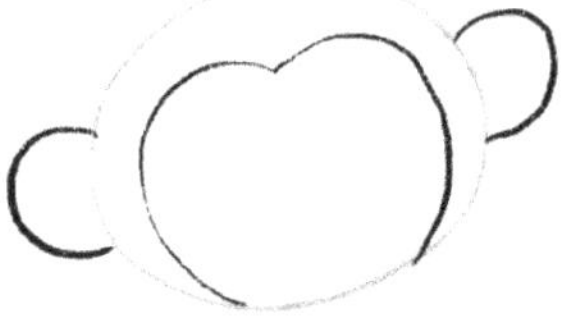

2

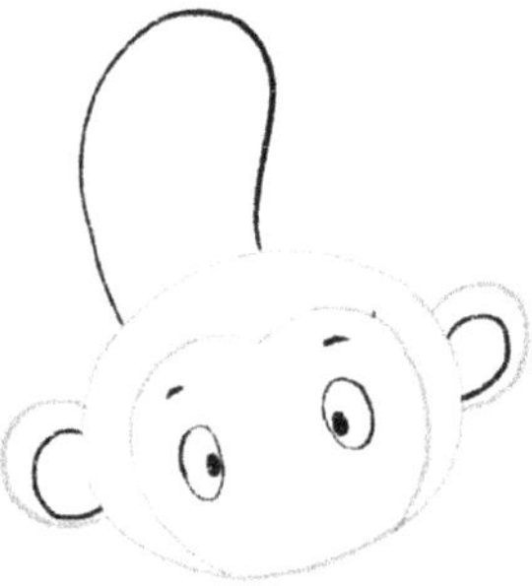

3

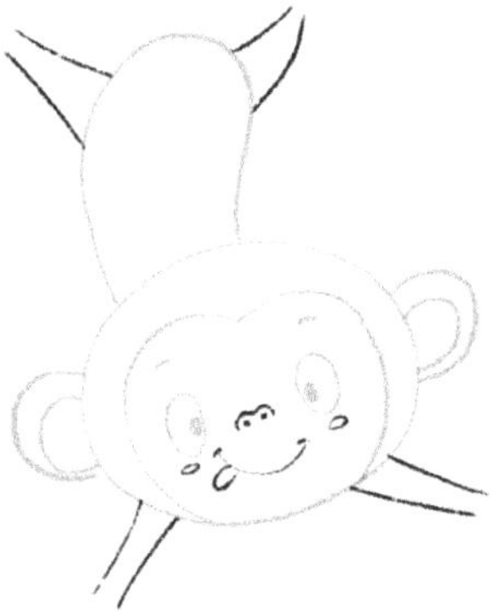

4

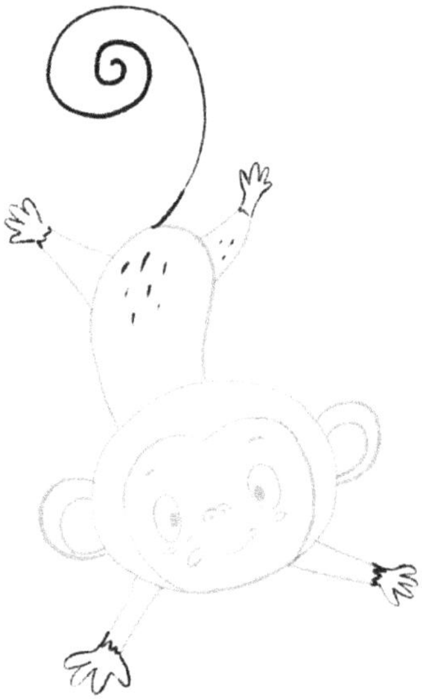

5

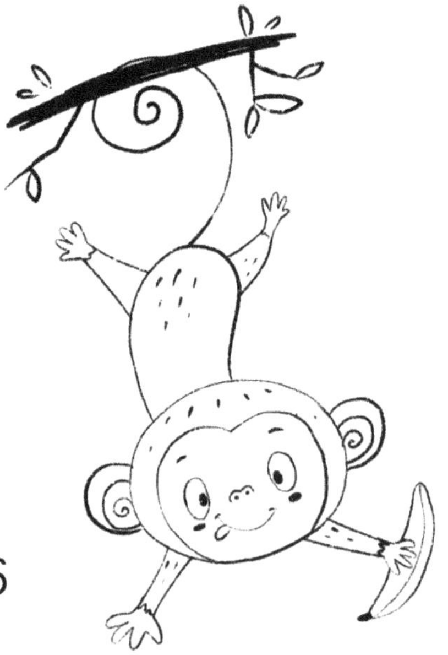

6

Practice here!

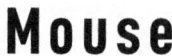

Mouse

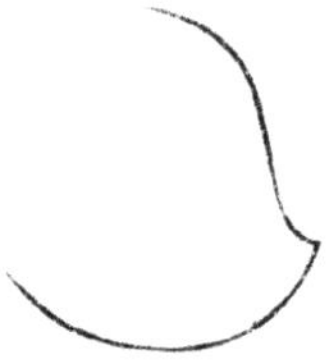

1

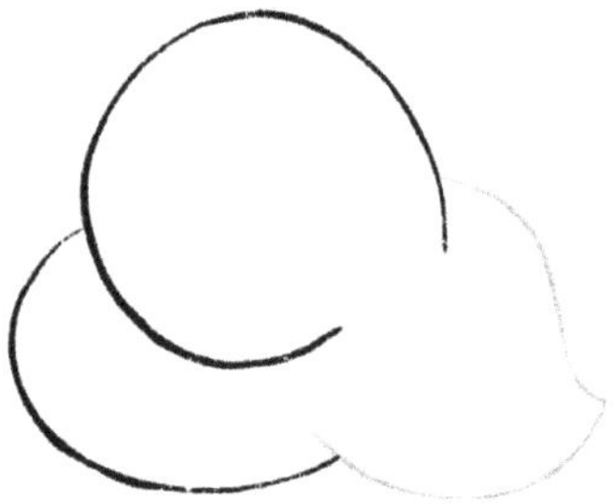

2

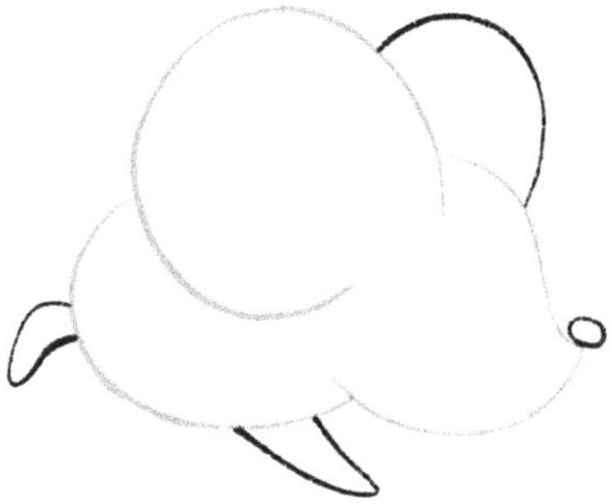

3

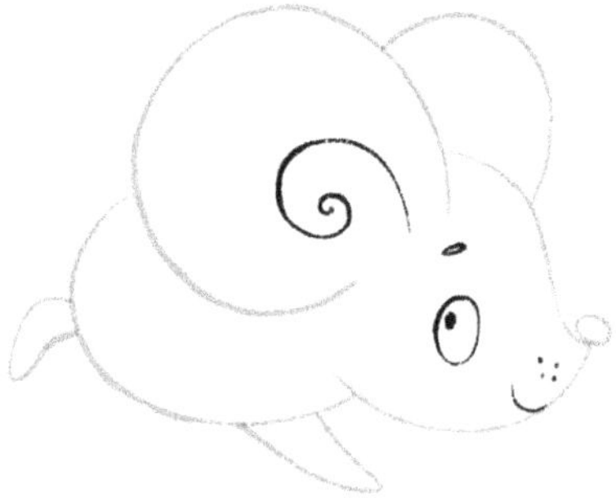

4

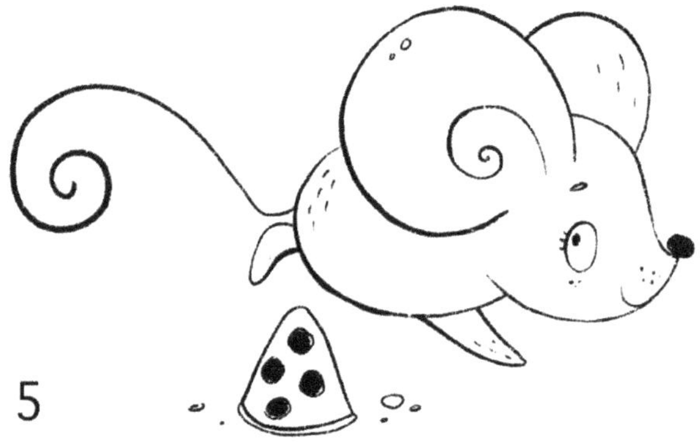

5

Practice here!

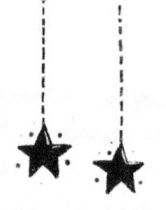

Owl

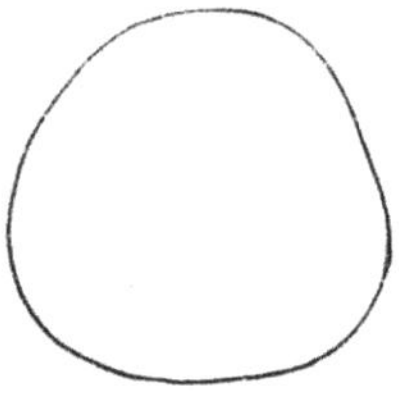

1

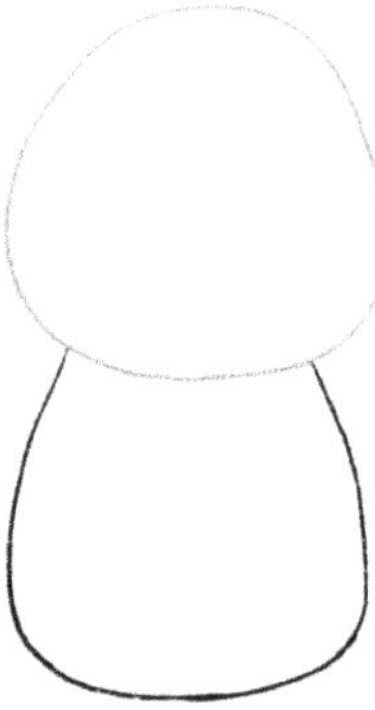

2

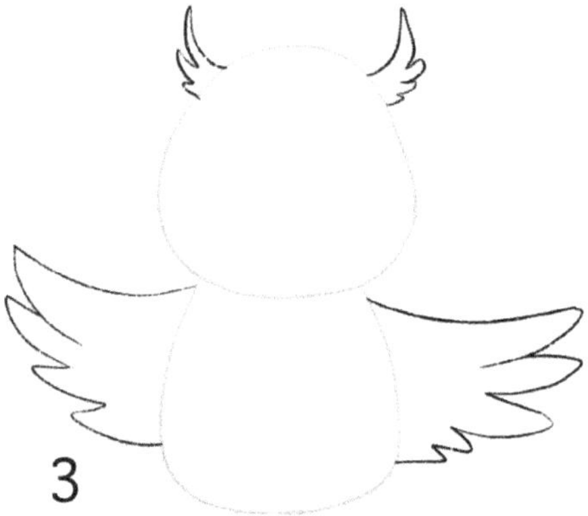

3

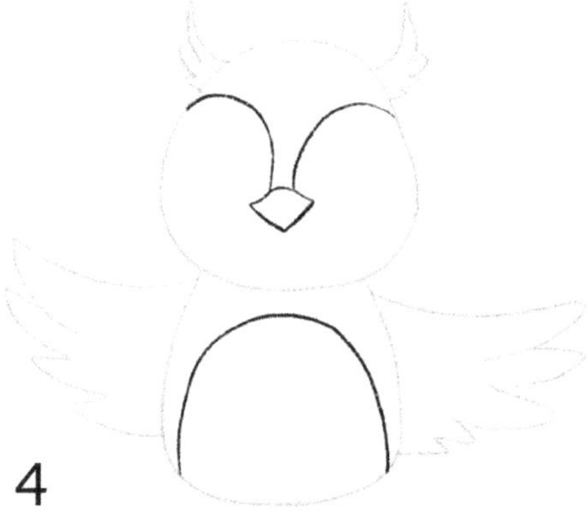

4

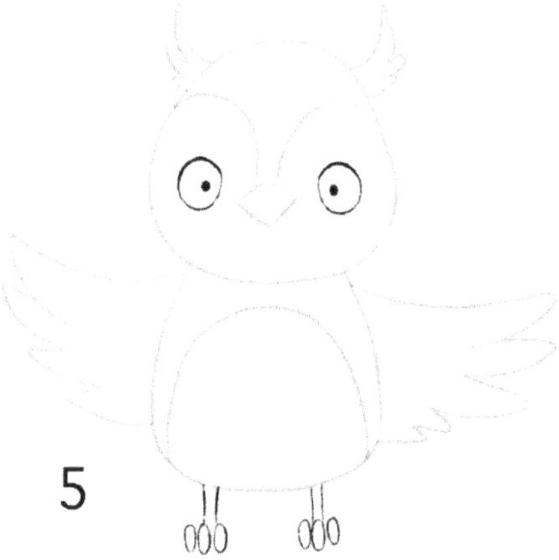

5

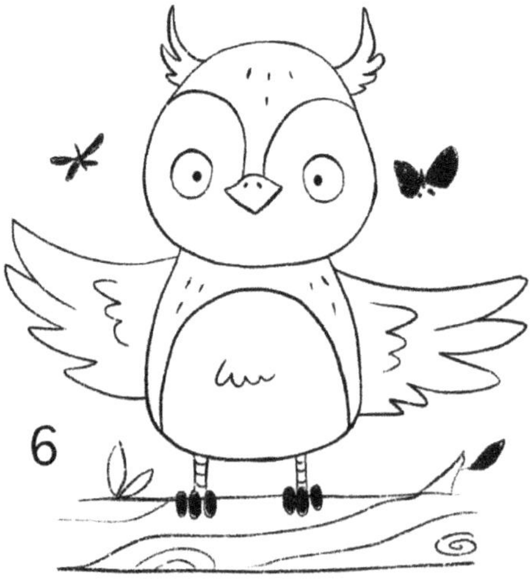

6

Practice here!

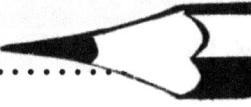

Panda

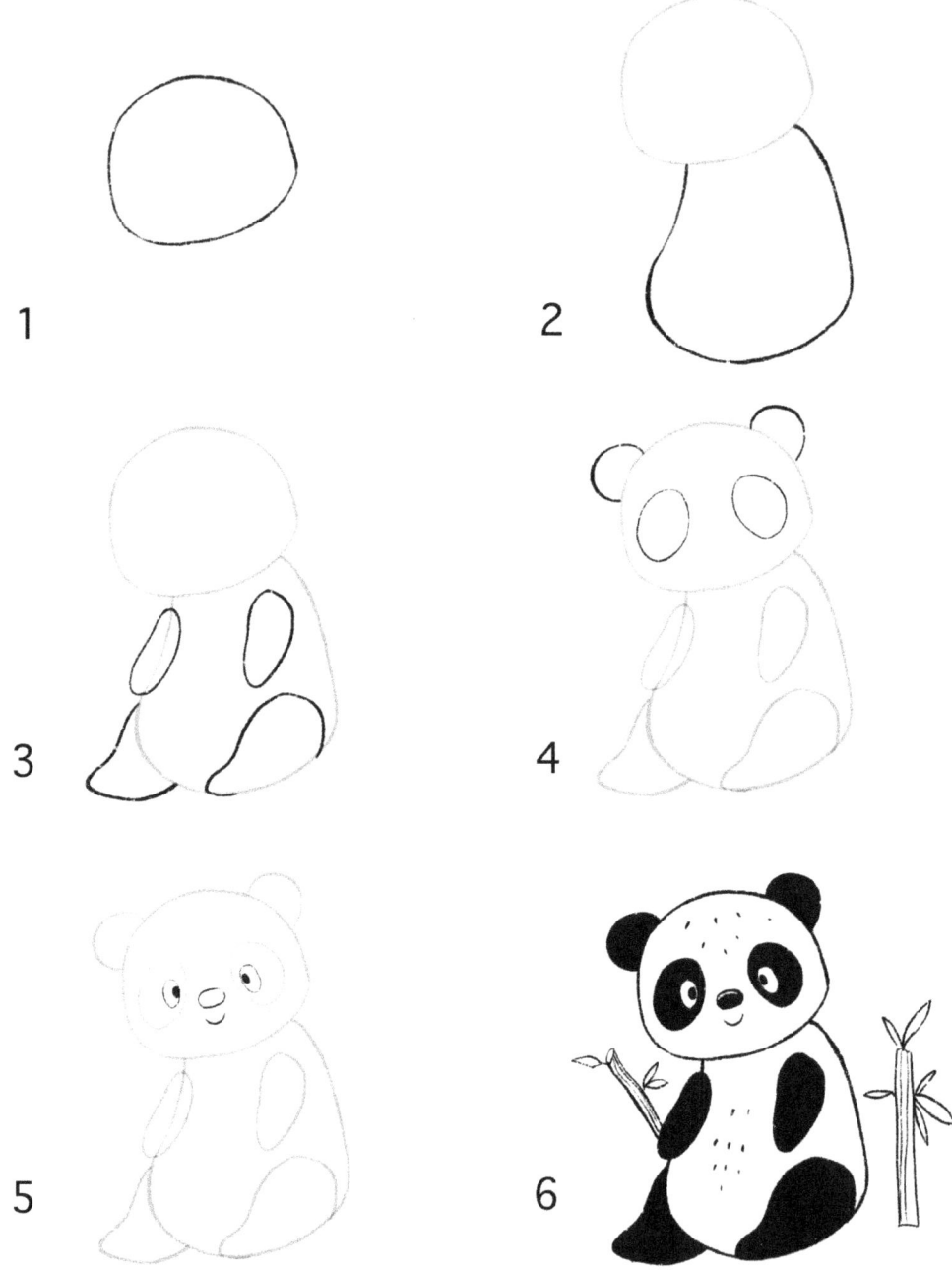

1

2

3

4

5

6

Practice here!

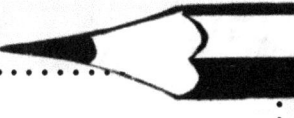

Penguin

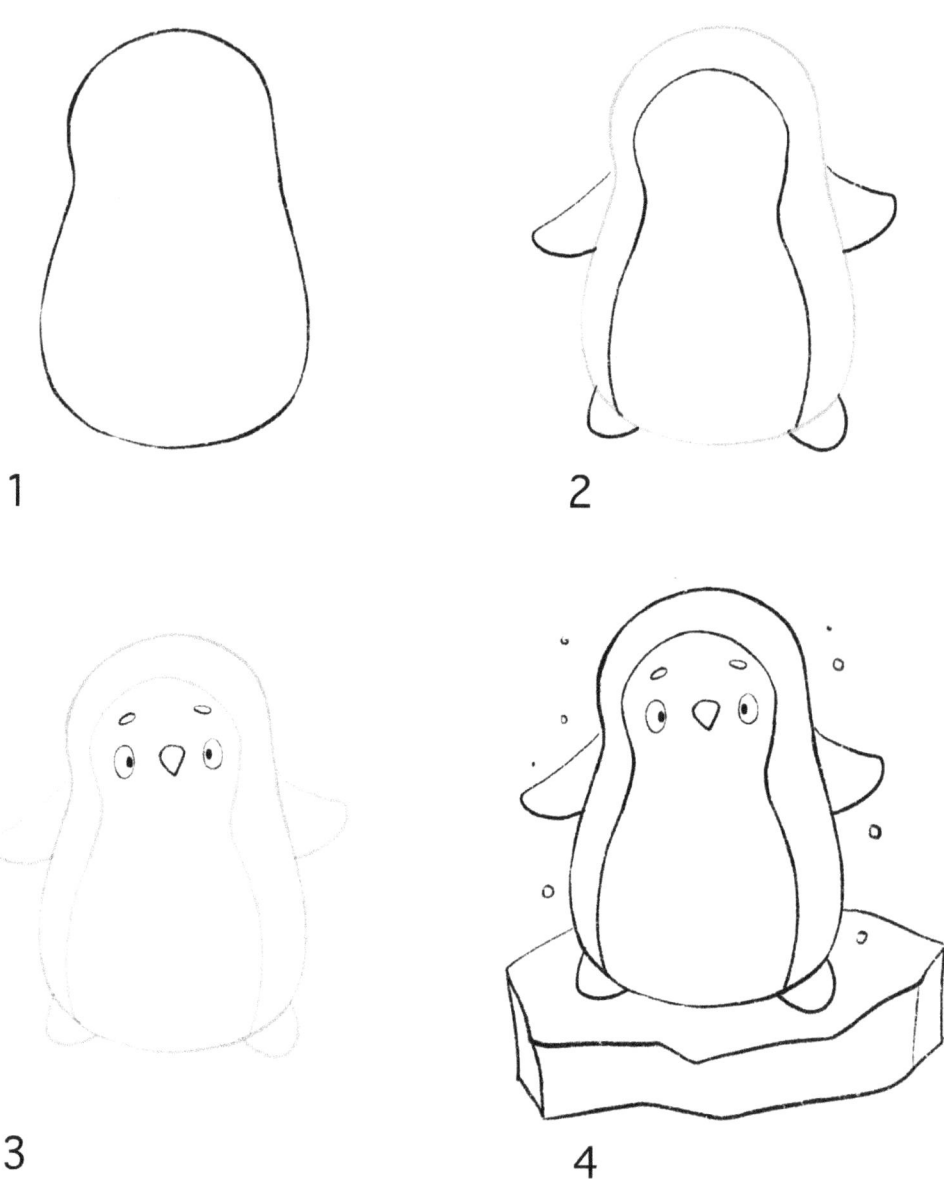

1

2

3

4

Practice here!

Pig

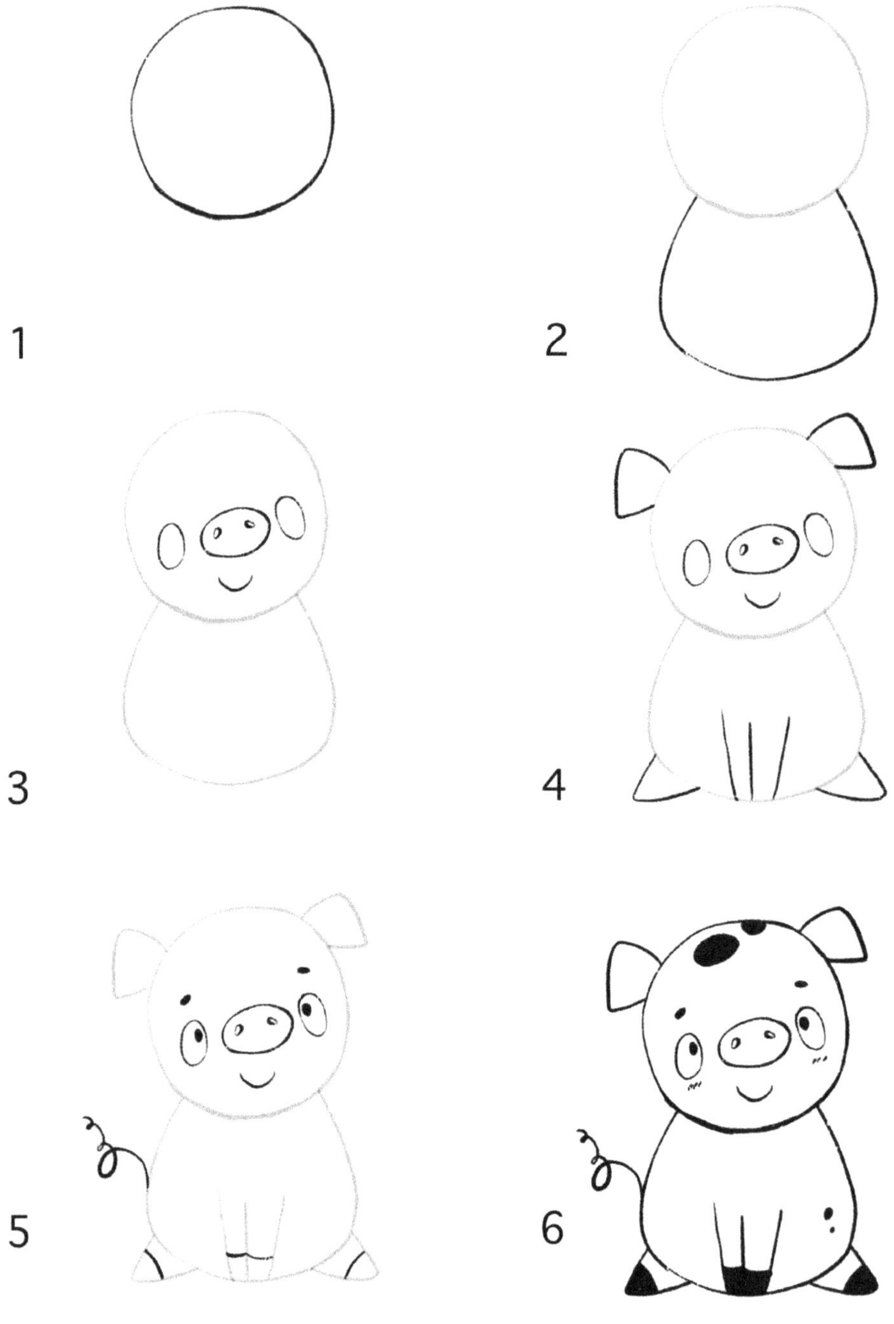

1

2

3

4

5

6

Practice here!

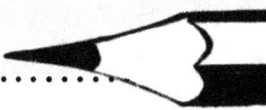

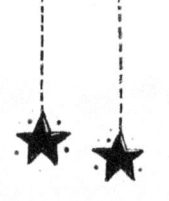

Rabbit

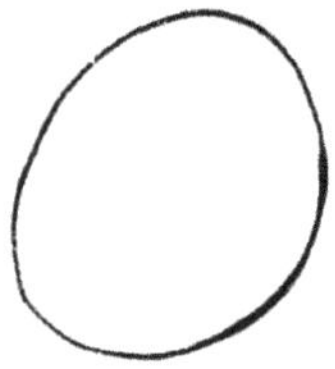

1

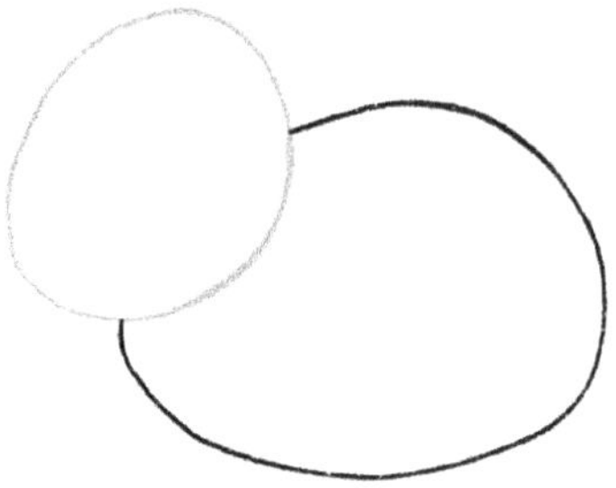

2

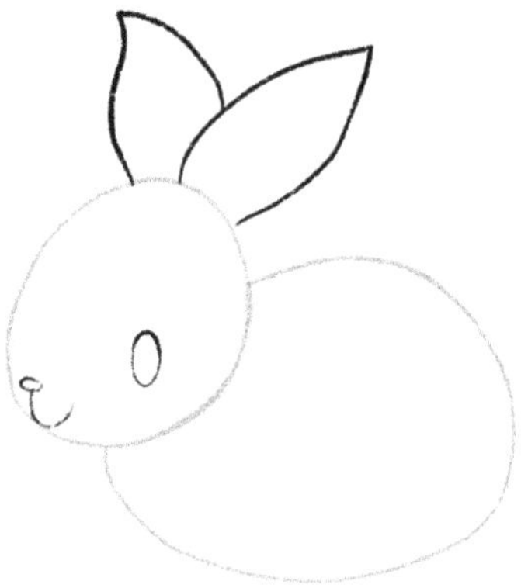

3

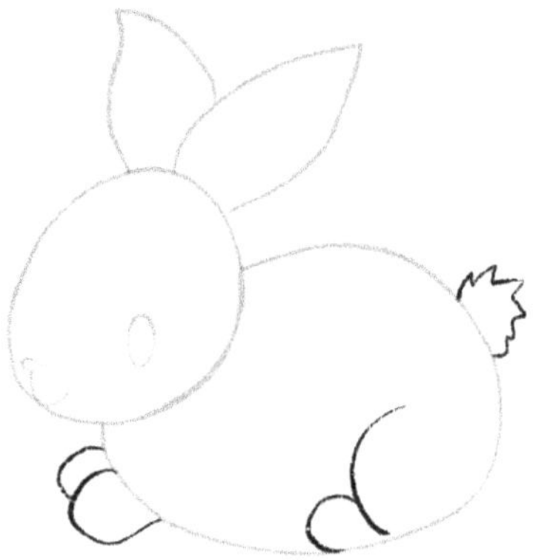

4

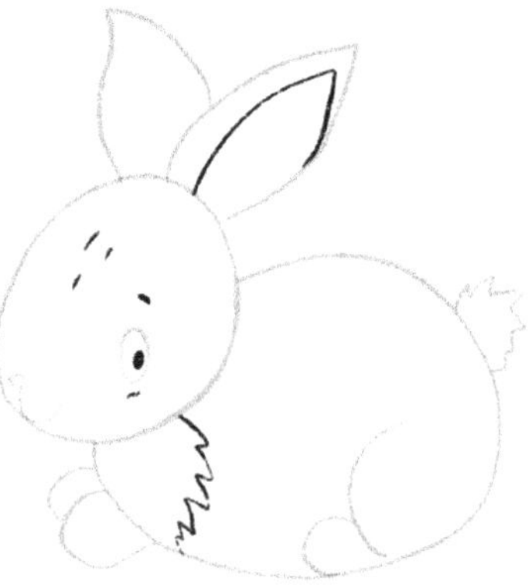

5

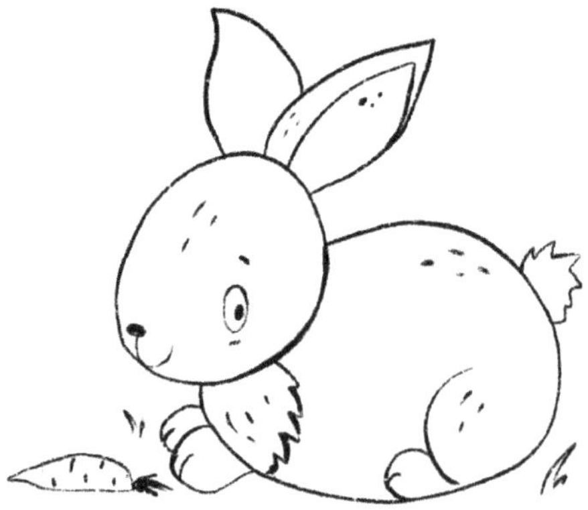

6

Practice here!

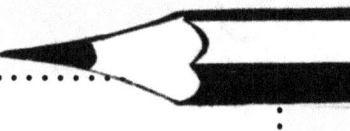

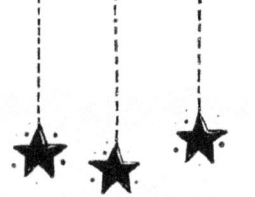

Raccoon

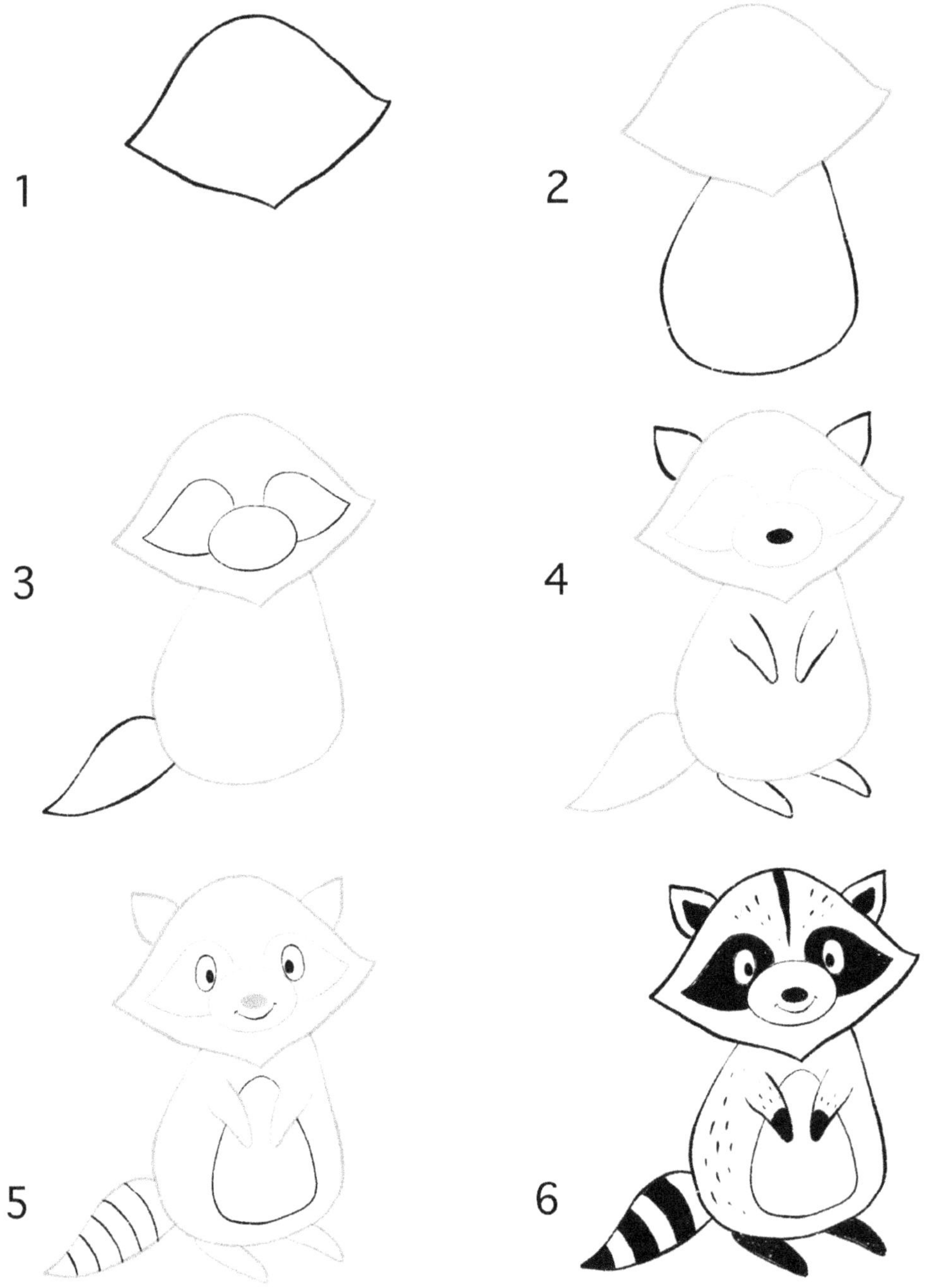

1

2

3

4

5

6

Practice here!

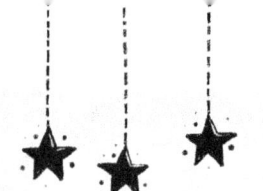

Rhino

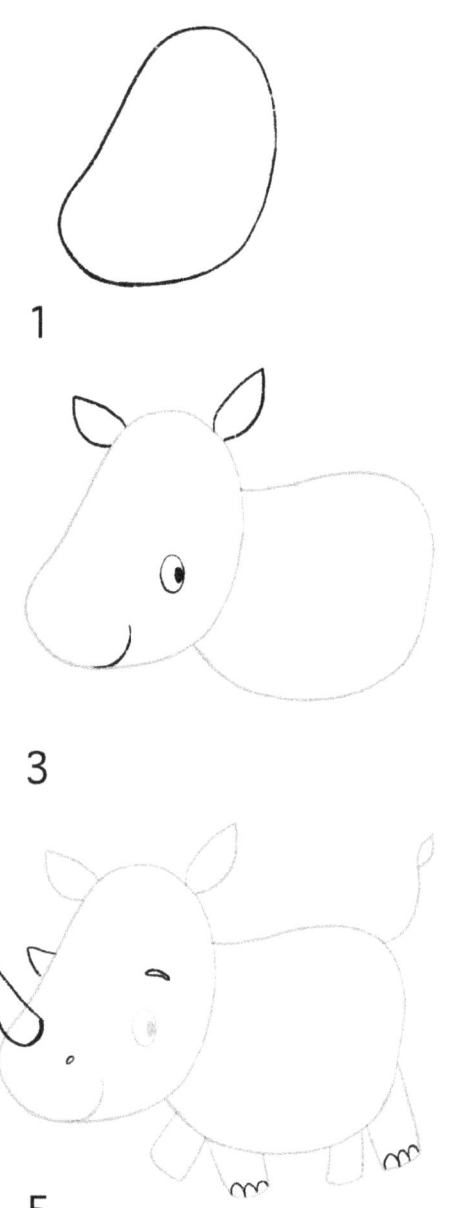

1

2

3

5

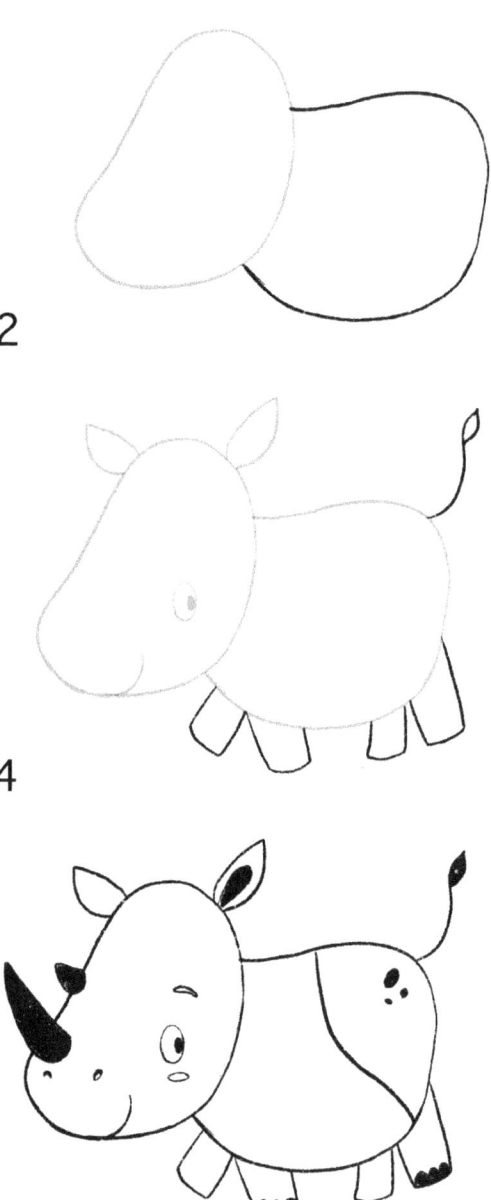

4

6

Practice here!

Seal

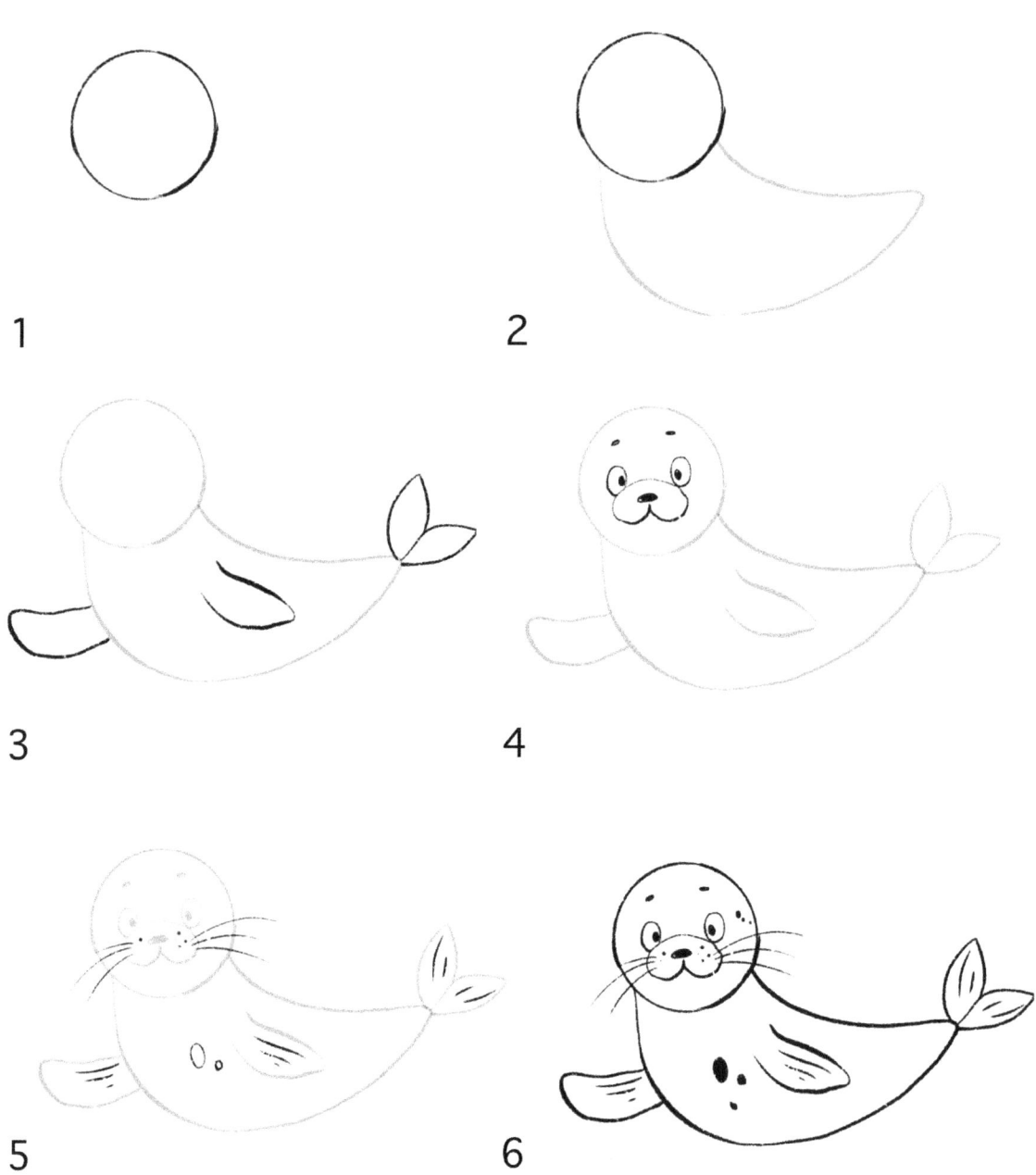

1

2

3

4

5

6

Practice here!

Shark

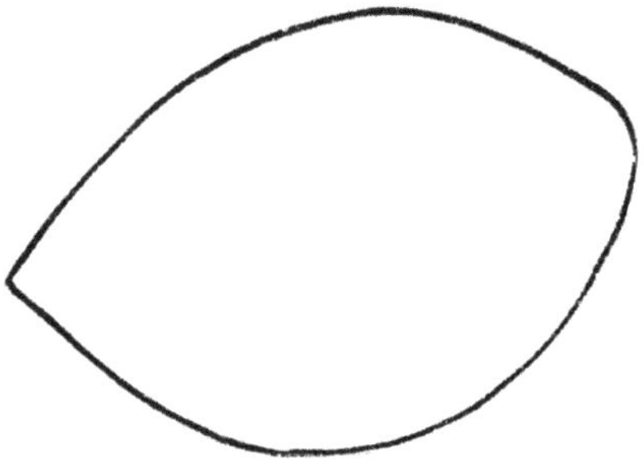

1

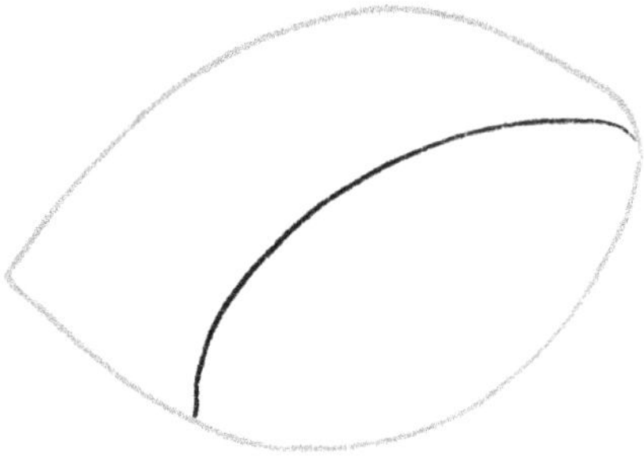

2

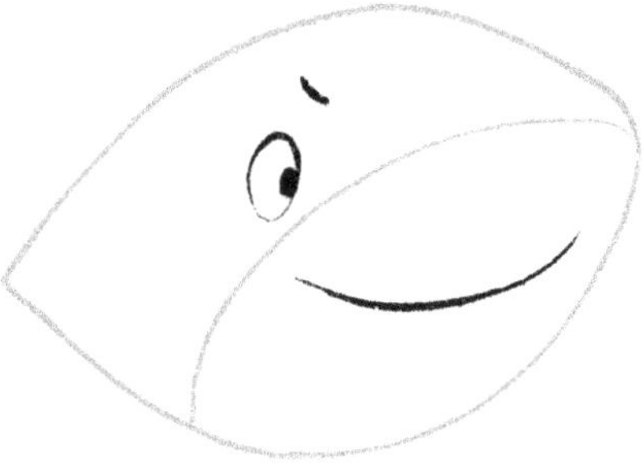

3

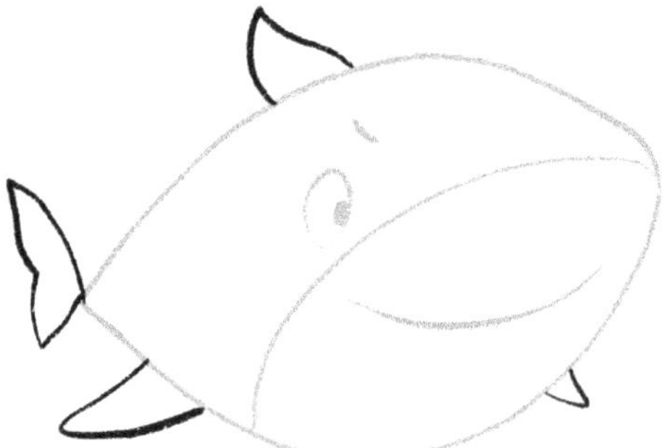

4

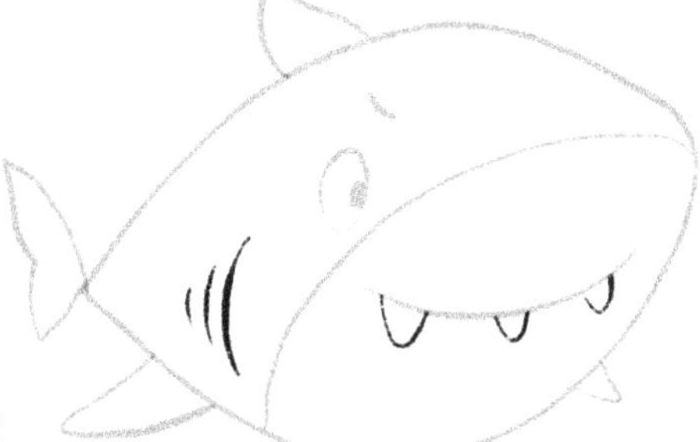

5

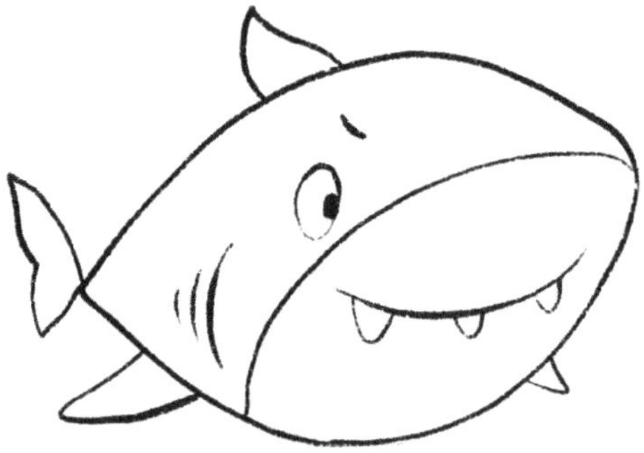

6

Practice here!

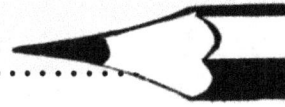

The first shape looks just like a lemon!

Sheep

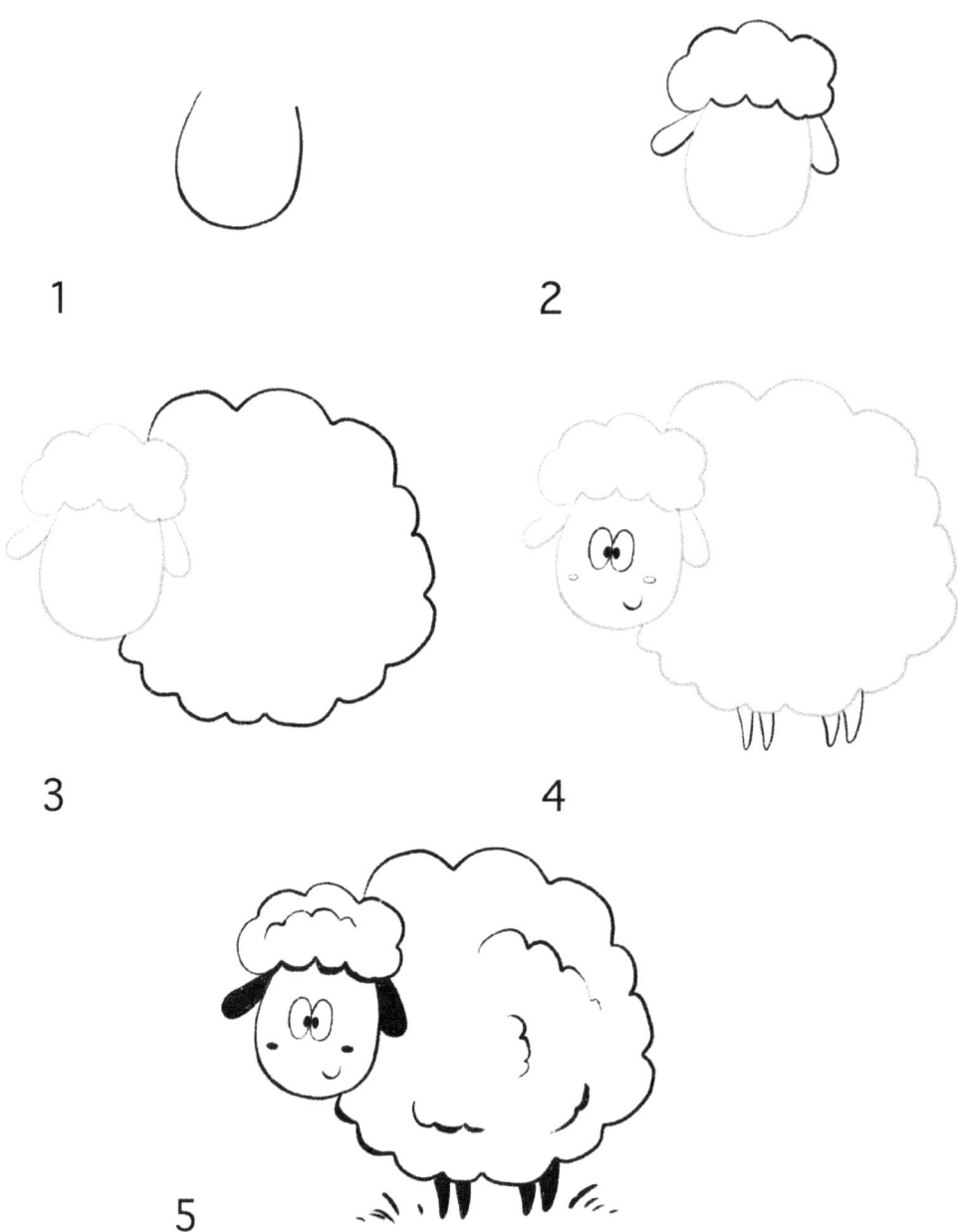

1

2

3

4

5

Practice here!

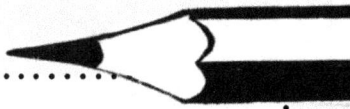

If you can draw a cloud - you can draw a sheep!

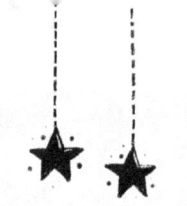

Sloth

1

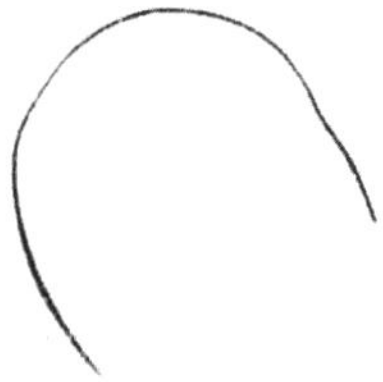

2

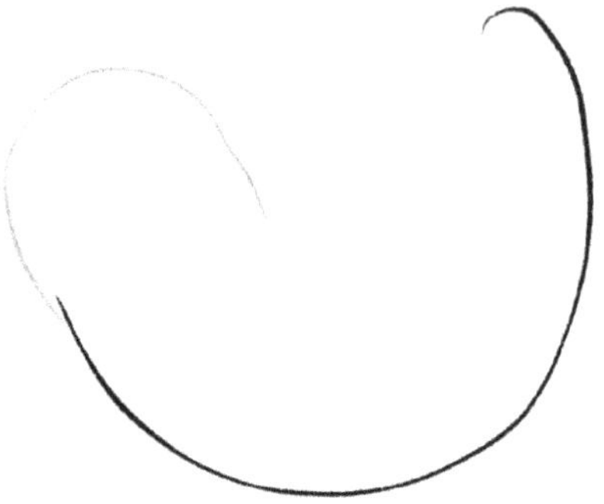

3

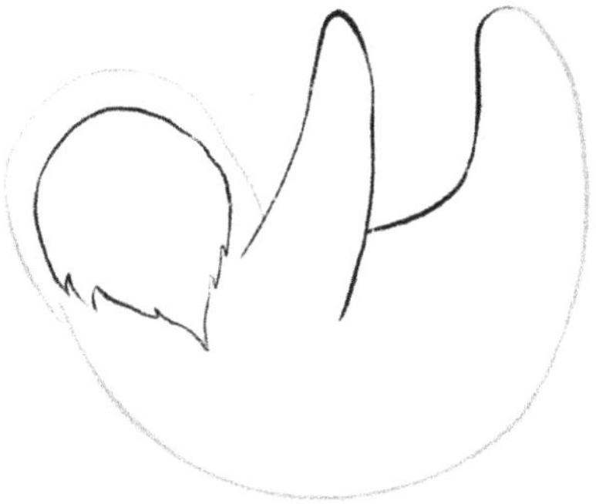

4

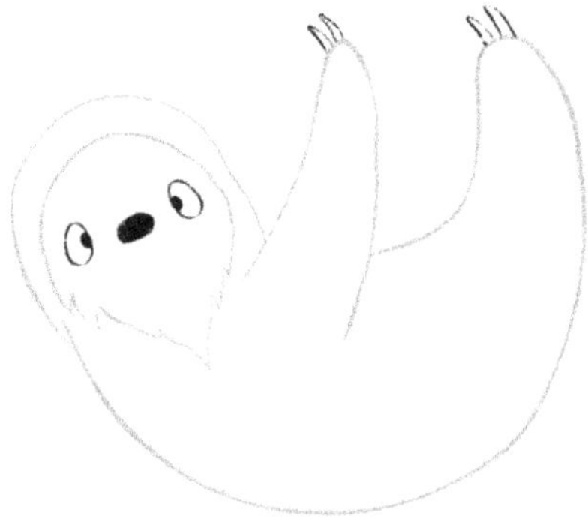

5

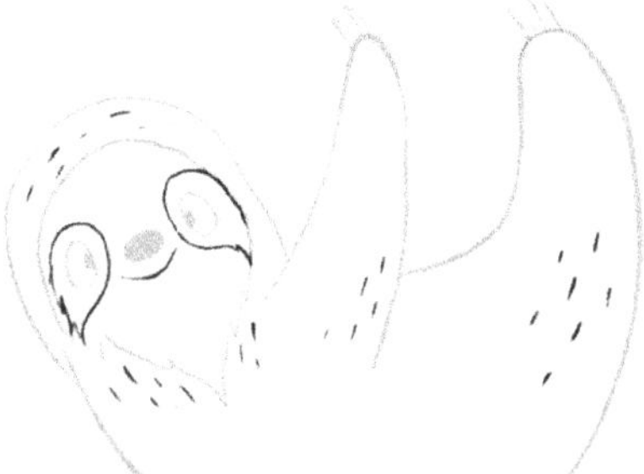

6

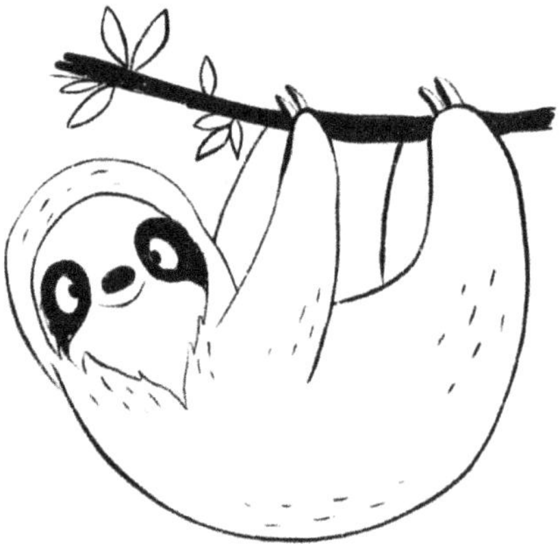

Practice here!

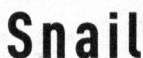

Snail

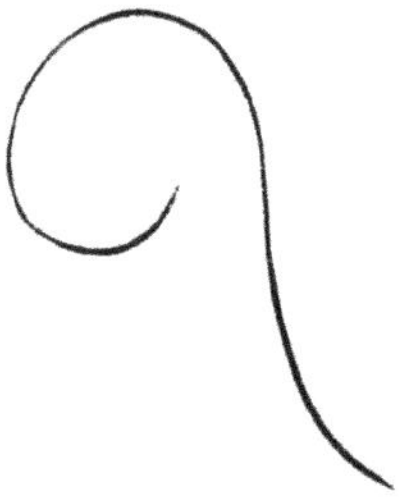

1

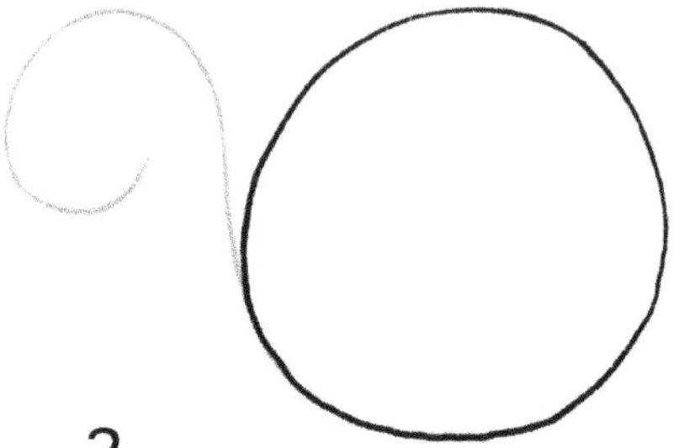

2

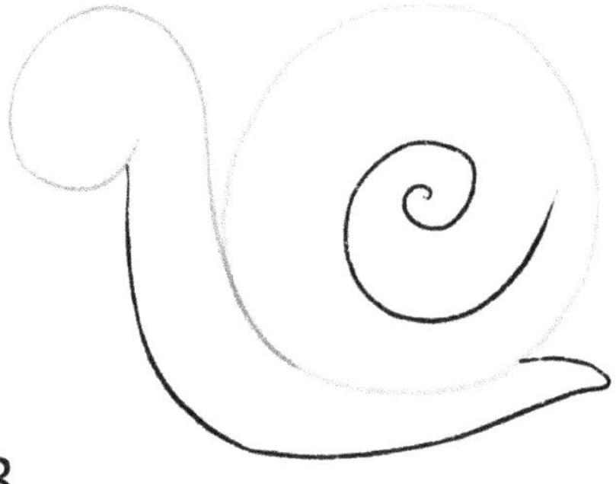

3

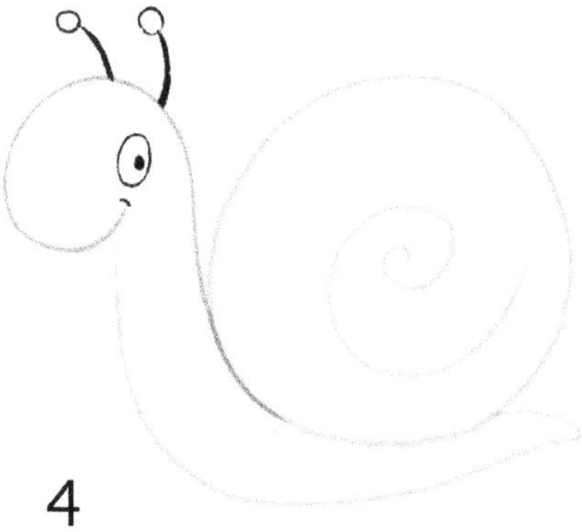

4

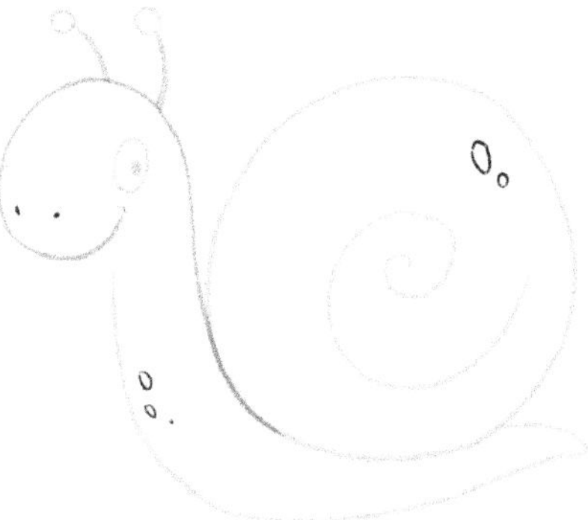

5

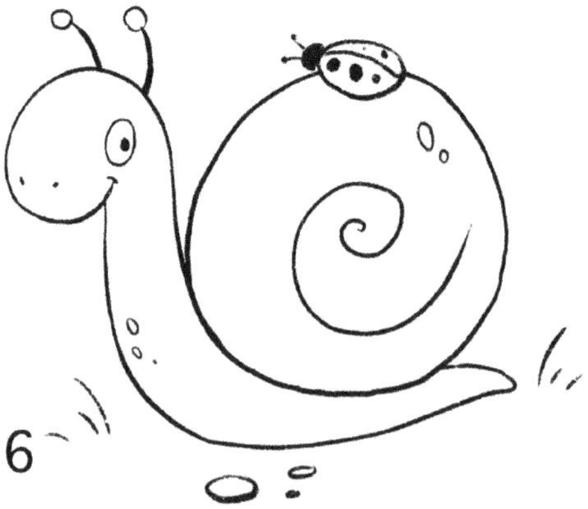

6

Practice here!

Sperm whale

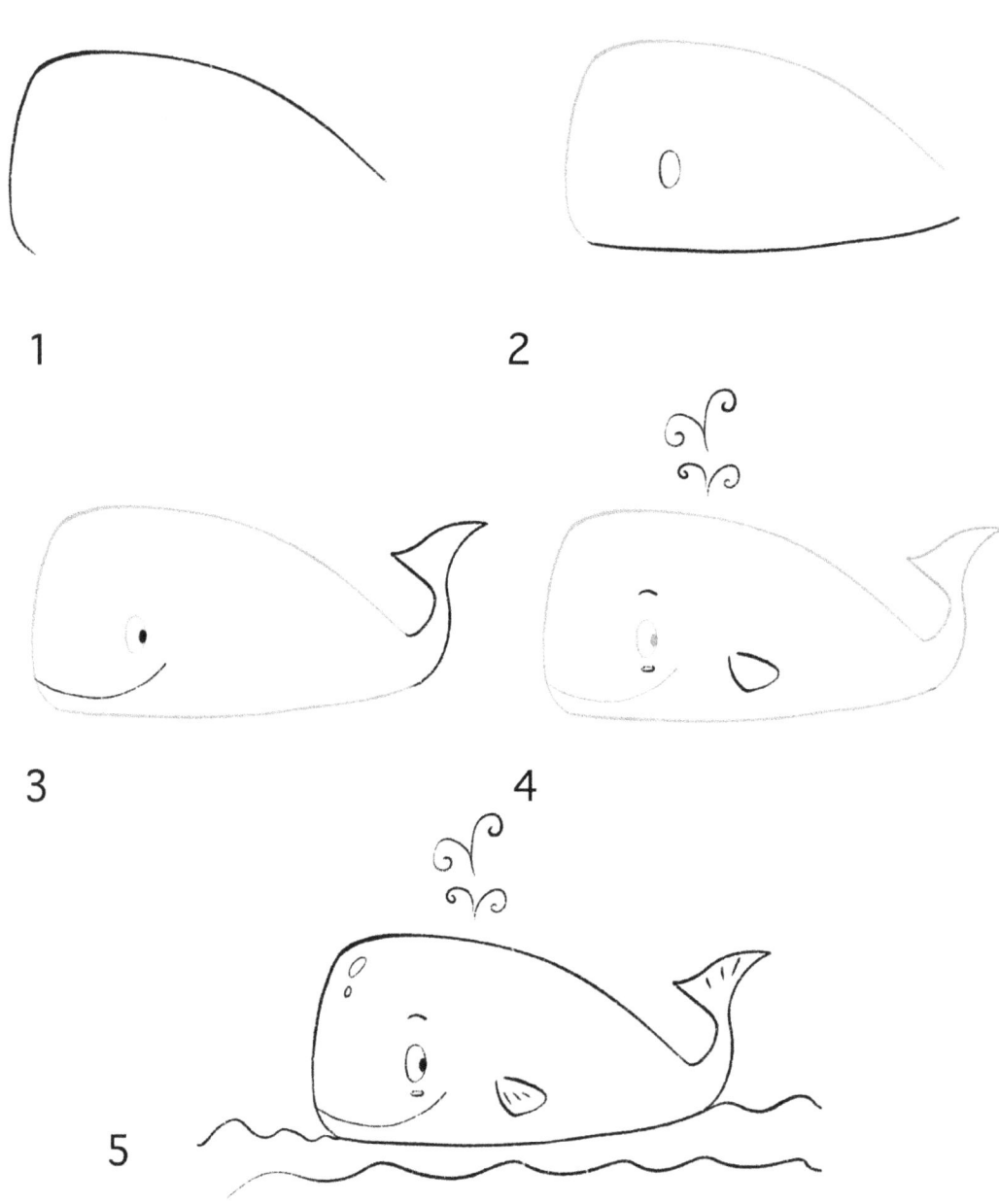

1

2

3

4

5

Practice here!

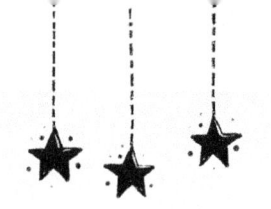

Squirrel

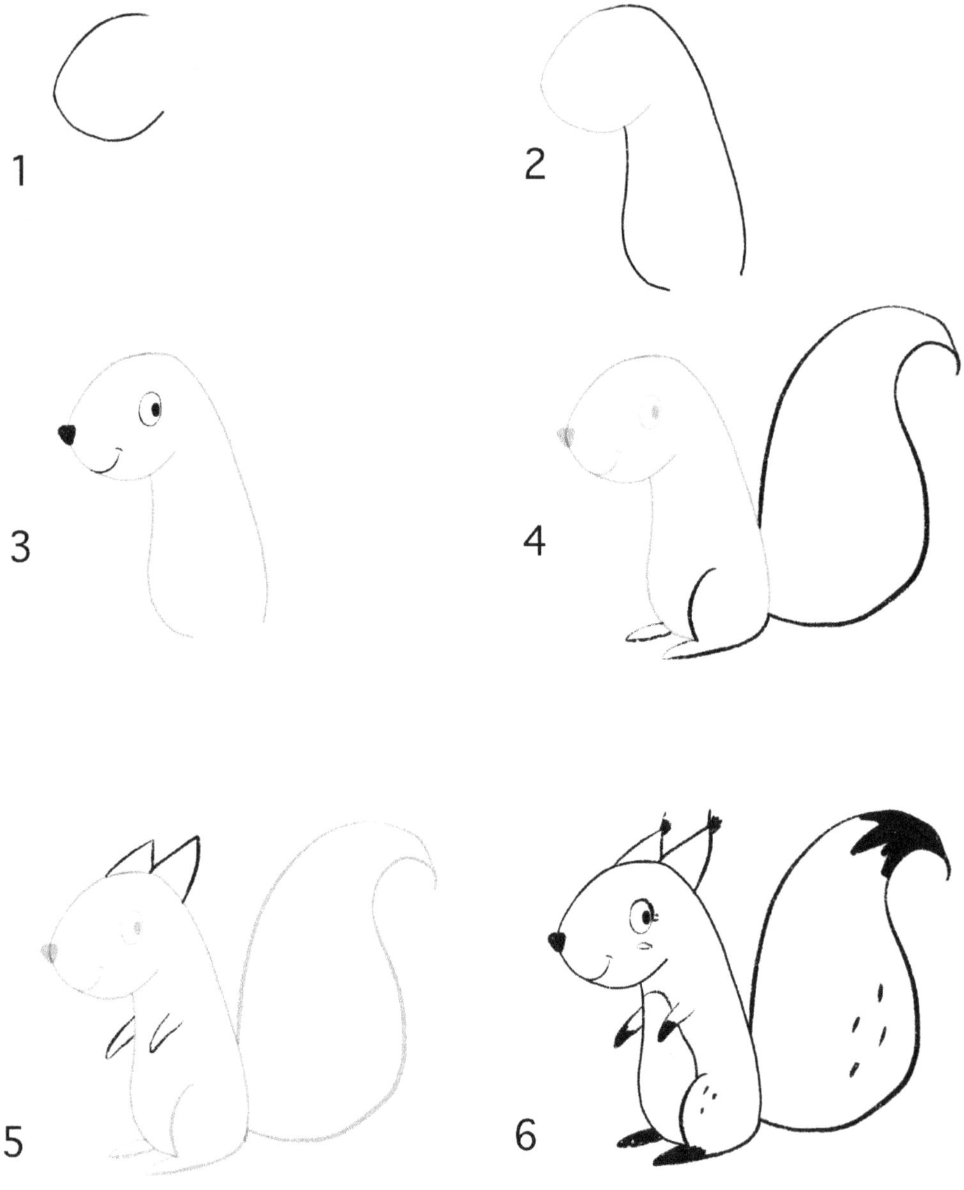

1

2

3

4

5

6

94

Practice here!

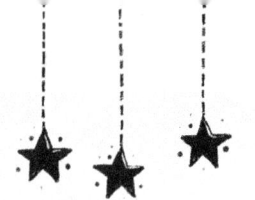

Tiger

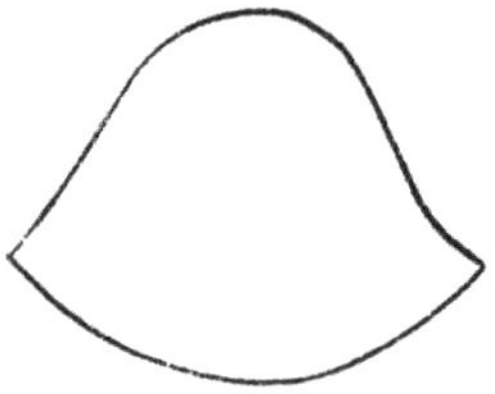

1

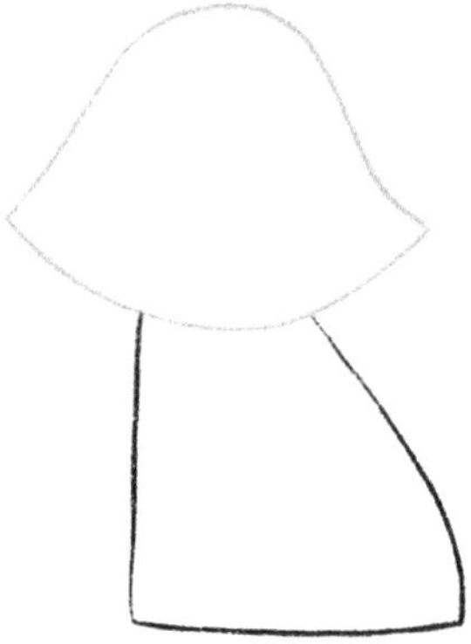

2

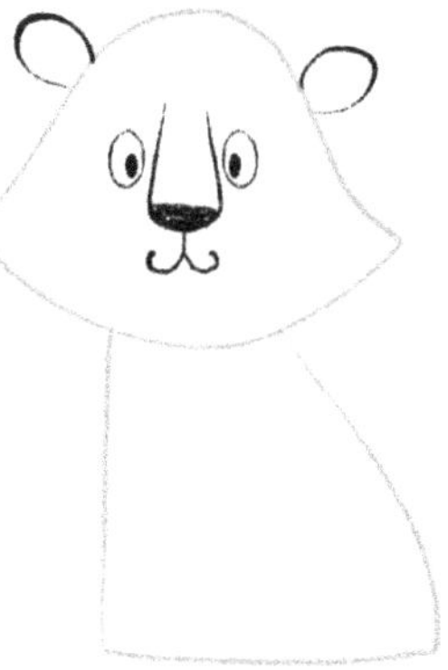

3

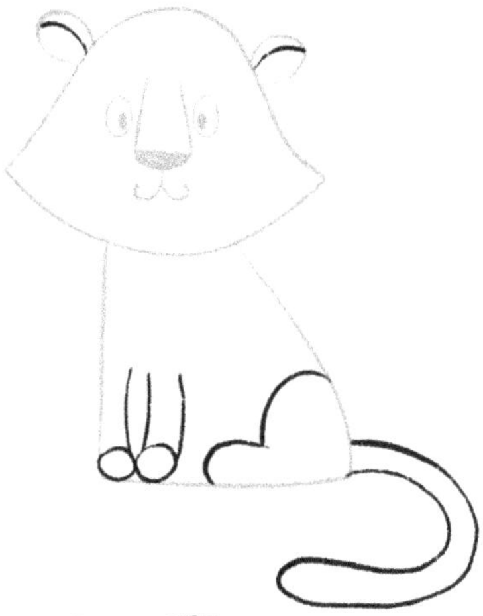

4

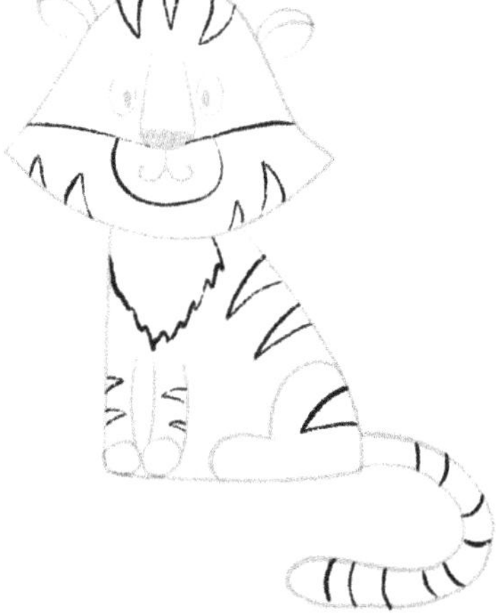

5

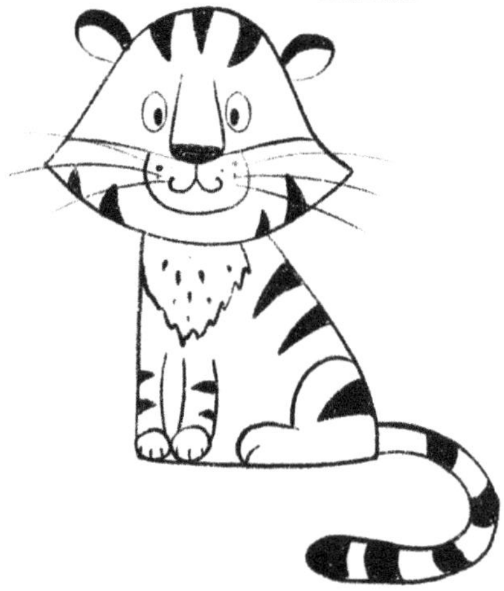

6

Practice here!

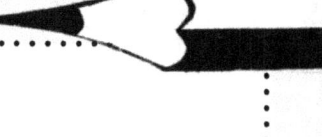

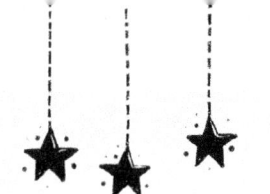

Turle

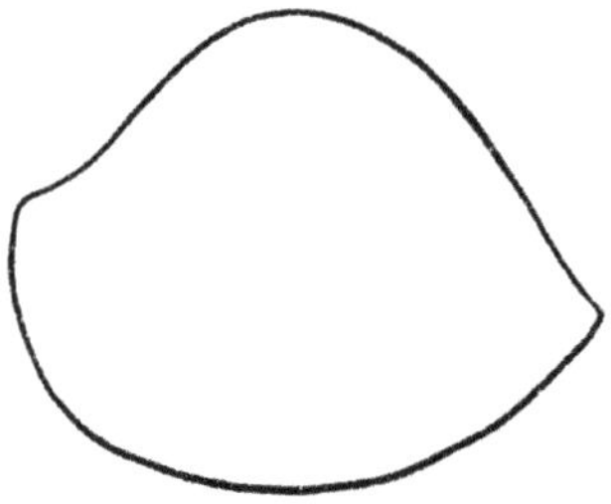

1

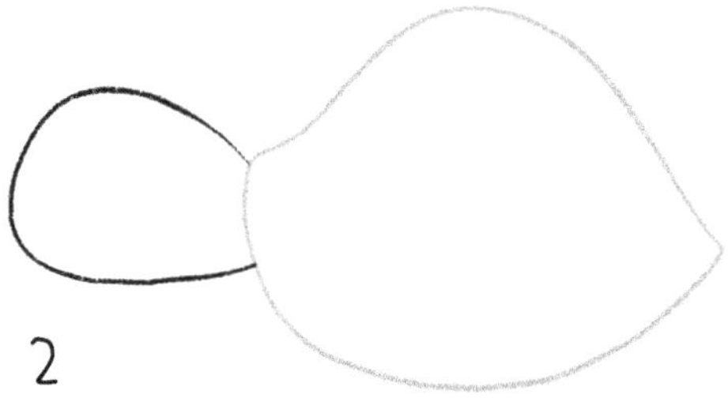

2

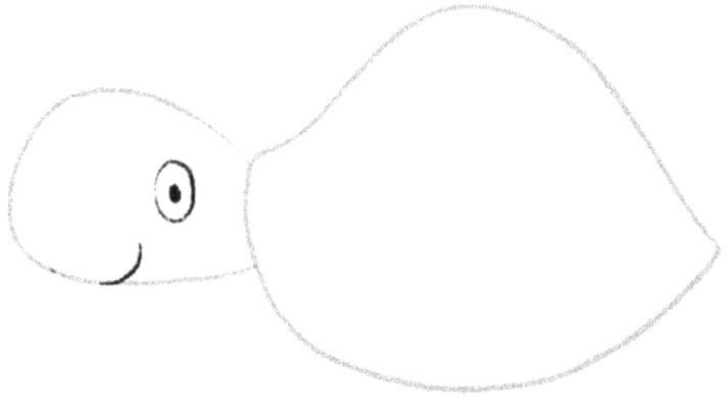

3

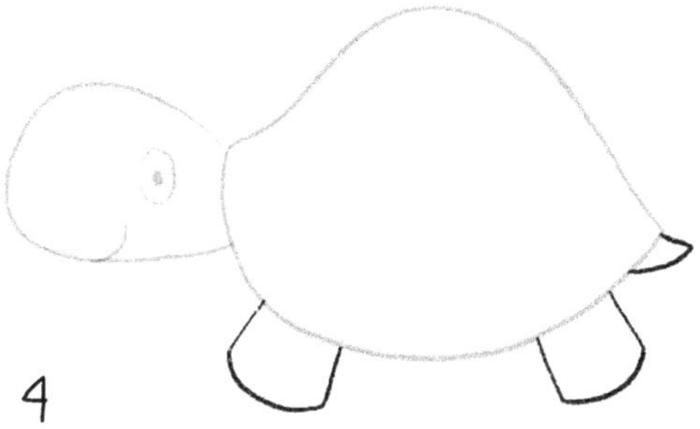

4

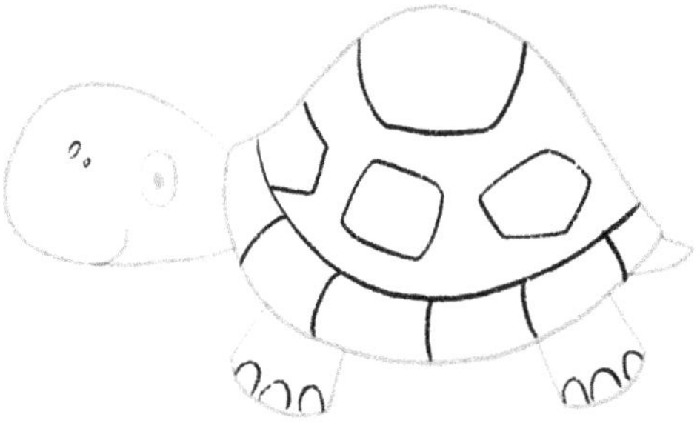

5

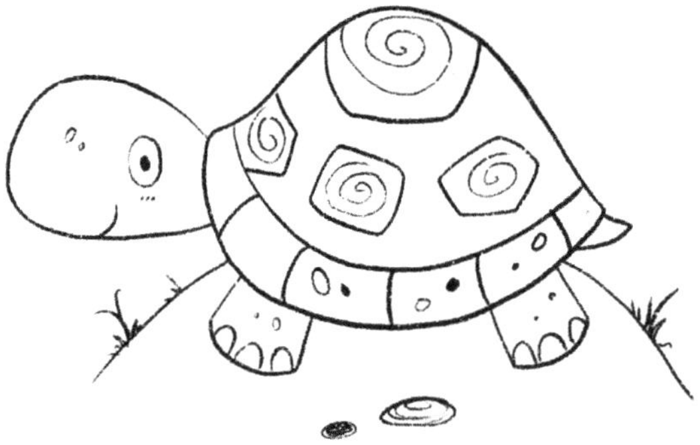

6

Practice here!

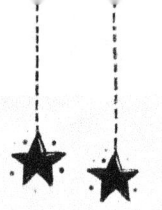

Whale

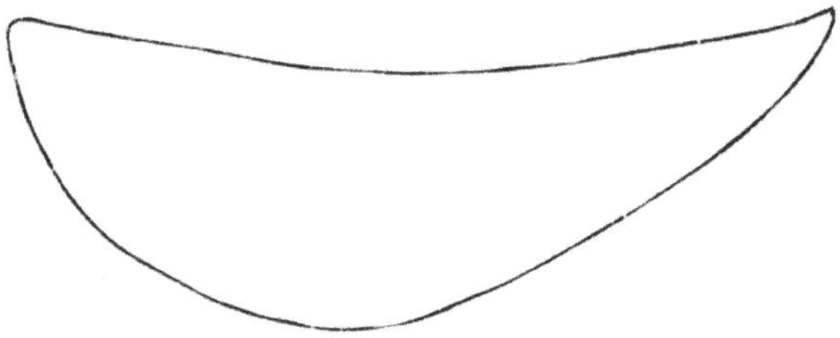

1

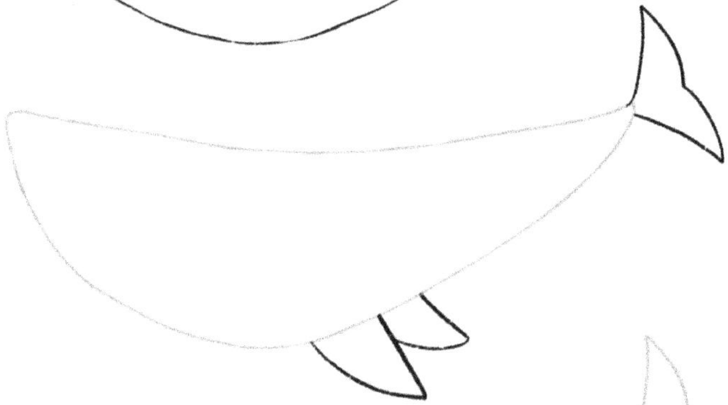

2

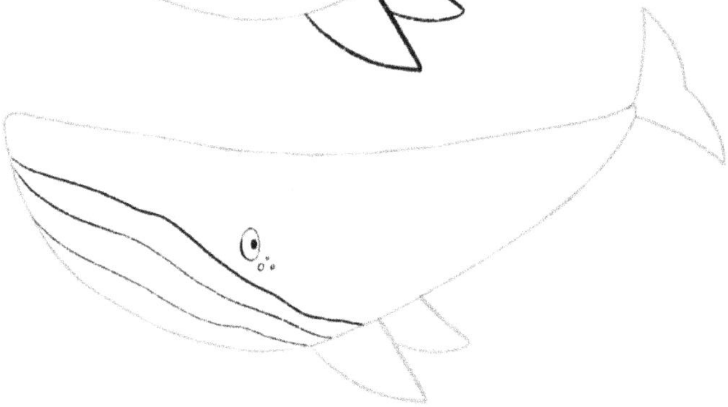

3

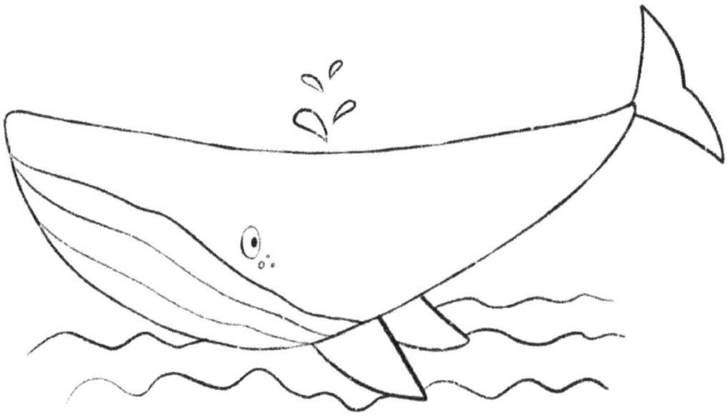

4

Practice here!

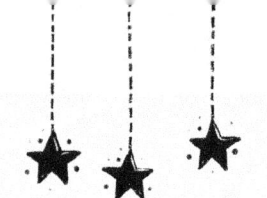

Wolf

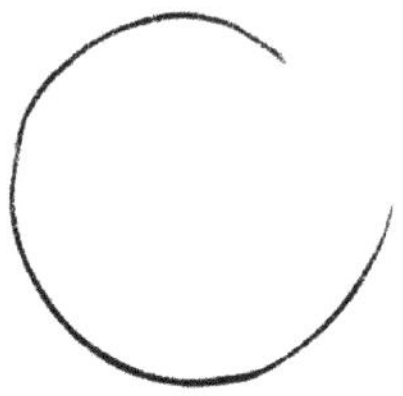

1

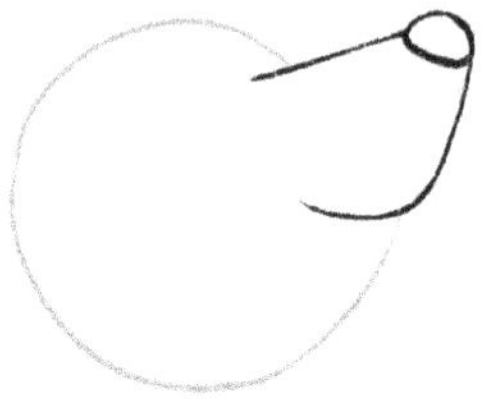

2

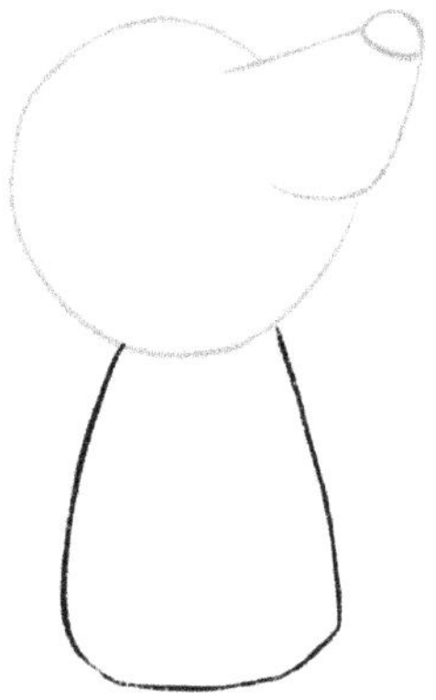

3

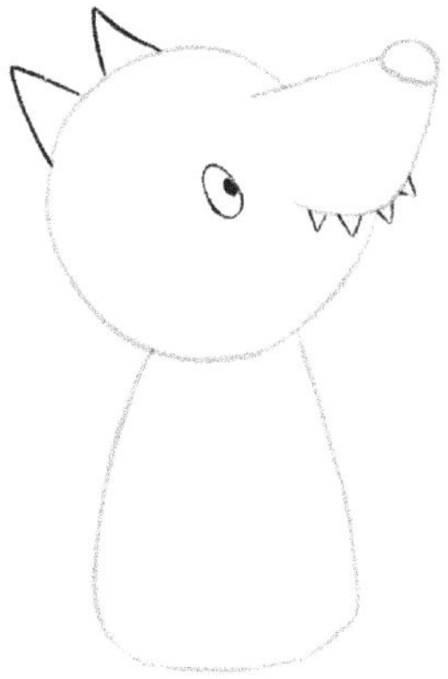

4

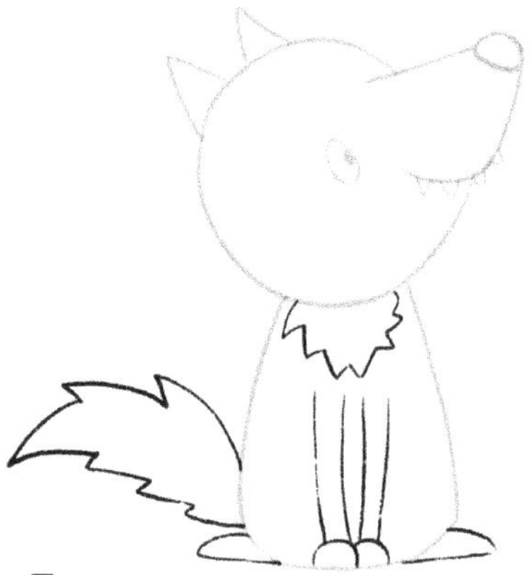

5

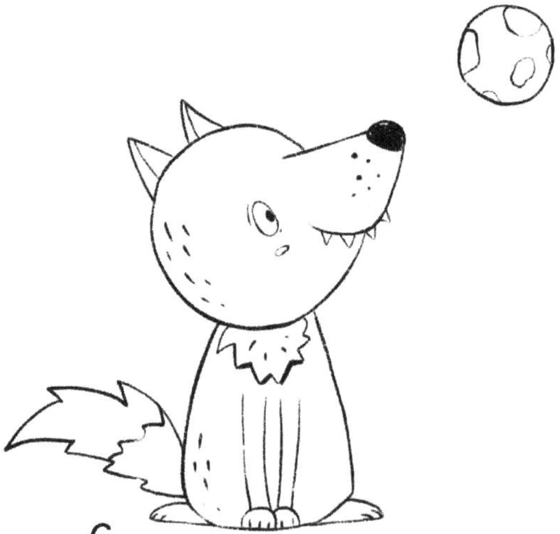

6

Practice here!

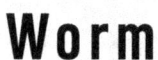

Worm

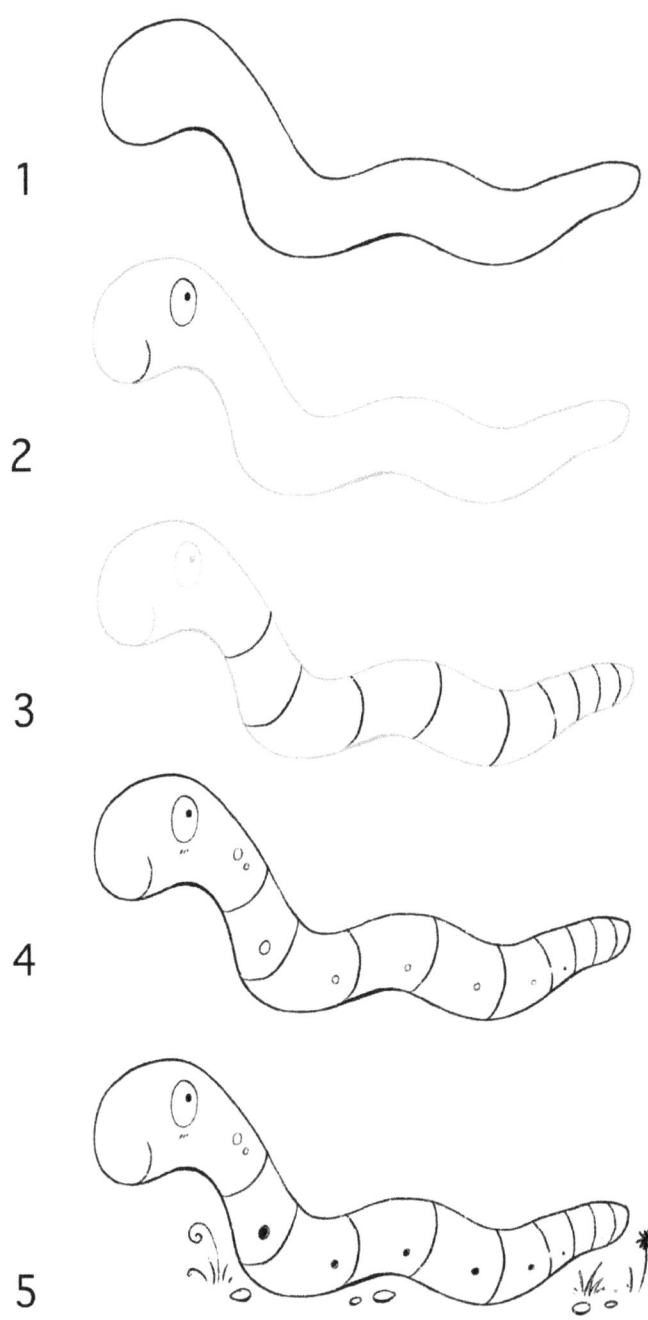

1

2

3

4

5

Practice here!

Practice here!

Hey!

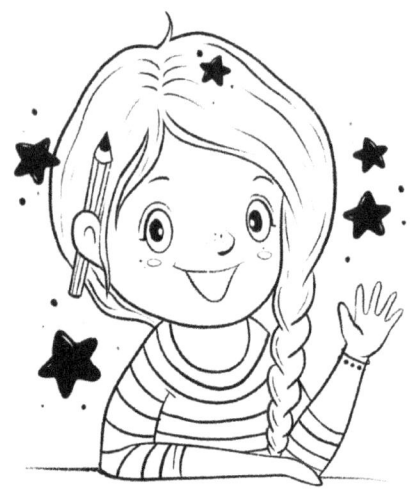

My name is Darya,
I'm the girl who
made this book.
Nice to meet you!

If you have any thoughts, suggestions, or
just want to say hi - feel free to contact me
via email - Darya-shch@hotmail.com
Also, don't hesitate to share your drawings!

If you enjoyed this book, please consider
giving us a review on Amazon. It helps more people
to discover our books and more kids to discover
their talent!

Thank you!

Get a free book!

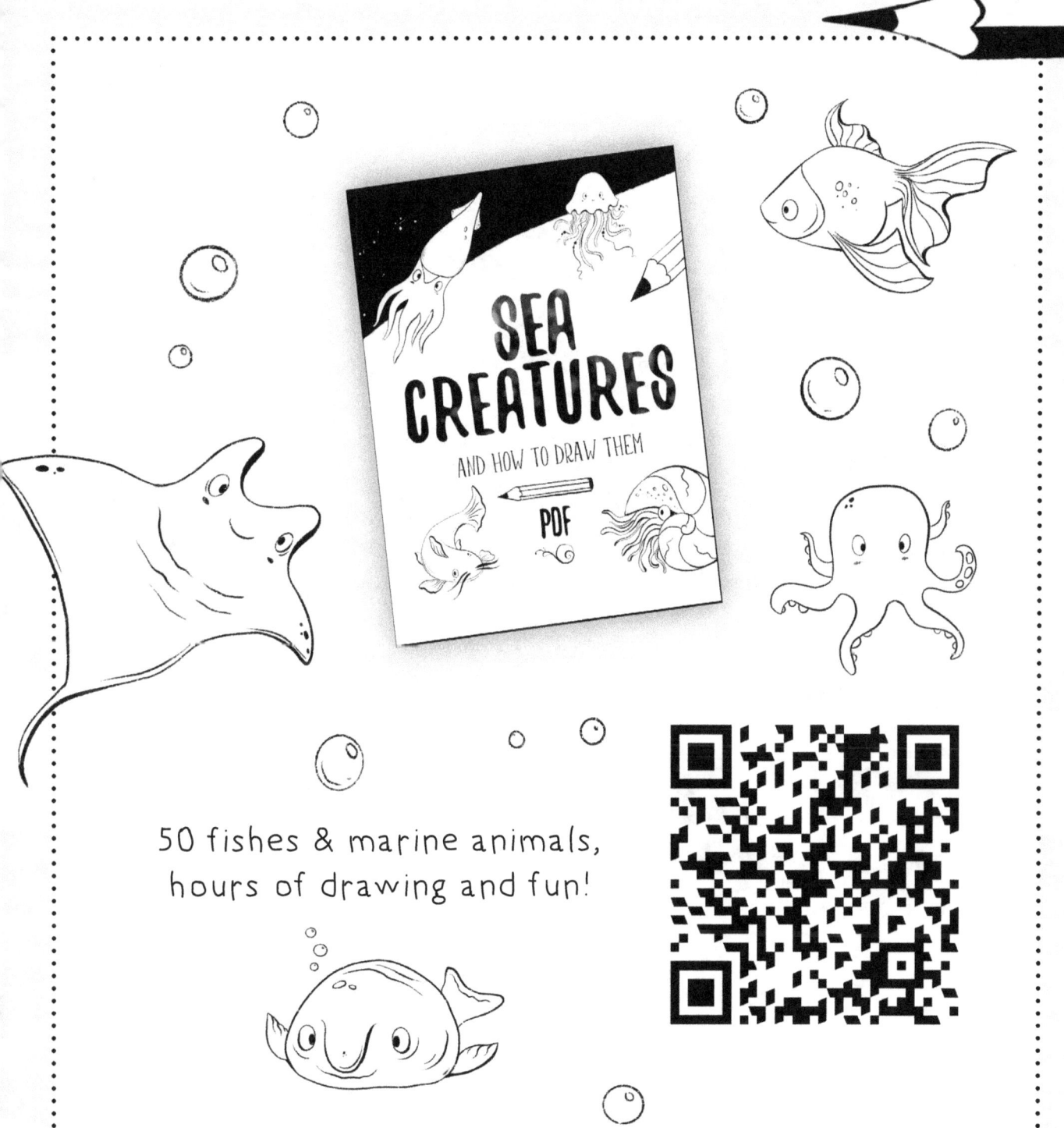

SEA CREATURES
AND HOW TO DRAW THEM
PDF

50 fishes & marine animals,
hours of drawing and fun!